Palate Passport

Neha Khullar

ISBN 978-0692939826

Palate Passport

ABOUT THE AUTHOR

Neha Khullar is a foodie, coffee addict, sparkly shoe-wearer, and enthusiastic dinner party host. Prior to becoming a cookbook author, Neha worked on the corporate side of New York City. Fueled by her passion for food and cooking, she set out on a journey to explore culinary traditions around the world.

After breaking bread in dozens of places, she learned that food brings people together and creates community regardless of religion, political views, or language; what tastes good can be shared with others. She has spent time with master chefs, street stall cooks, grandmothers, and food lovers all around the world. They have taught her about their favorite local foods and shared the history and stories behind them. Palate Passport is her personal culinary masterpiece created to share this journey with others. She intends to show readers that cooking is fun, it doesn't have to be intimidating, and if made with love, even an imperfect dish will taste beautiful!

Neha has spent three years creating this book in order to thoughtfully coordinate all of its components. The cover was inspired by many people and separate events. After following a particular artist for years, she asked him to create the cover art, loving his style of coloring outside of the lines–a style reminiscent of her story for creating this cookbook. The dominant colors of the cover were inspired by a garden that Neha visited in Marrakech, Morocco. And the name was inspired by a fellow traveler who crossed paths with Neha while also filling her passport with experiences. Every component of this book has a story like the one behind the cover art.

Neha is the founder of Food Moodz, LLC which is an online platform for foodies to share articles on the best eats, chef profiles, recipes, and food trends. Neha is also the founder of Global Foodie Citizens which is a community of foodies located all around the world! The vision for GFC is to offer an invite-only group of foodies who can connect to meet at exclusive restaurants and food experiences around the world.

INTRODUCTION

A lifetime. I've said that it has taken me 3 years to write this book. It has actually taken me a lifetime.

As a child travel was fun, and a time that I got to eat all those things that I loved but didn't get enough of at home–burgers, cheesesteaks, and really anything that involved meat and cheese. What I looked forward to was that each meal would be eaten at a different restaurant and sometimes in a different city. I didn't care that we were standing on Giant's Causeway in Northern Ireland or taking in Niagara Falls in Canada or in the presence of one of the oldest symbols of love in the world, the Taj Mahal. I didn't care about the history surrounding me or the aura of the part of the world that I was in – I cared about our next meal.

Travel as a young professional right out of college meant hitting all of the party towns with friends. I certainly had my fair share of local cuisine during this time period, but most of that included food I had at 3 a.m. after a night of hurricane drinks in Louisiana, USA, champagne bottles in Paris, France, or bucket drinks at the full moon party in Koh Phangan, Thailand.

When I started making a better living, I traveled to stay at the best places, dine at the most expensive restaurants, and take pictures next to all of the landmarks where I traveled as a way to capture memories and more importantly, to show off to friends and family.

In my late 20s and early 30s, I started traveling for the experience. I began exploring spirituality and it slowly crept into the way I viewed everything, taking me beyond surface level. By this time, things had happened – I had break-ups, lost friends, and my family started having major health issues. I started facing the demons within me. What I noticed during this phase was that many people around me couldn't tell that I was going through so much. To most people, I was a very happy person who was privileged to travel more often than most.

Though inside I was troubled. Because of that, I paid attention to details and I listened to everyone and anyone who spoke to me. I became, and still am, very sensitive to emotions. A beautiful thing happened during this time. I started to appreciate the little things – a smile, a friendly chat, an exchange about favorite foods. Most of all, I became humble and started peeling off my layers to become my authentic self. Travel opened up my eyes and showed me how I was a product of my surroundings. My truth and reality was completely different than a person's reality in Istanbul, Turkey or any other place around the world.

One thing was consistent throughout every phase of my travels and experiences. I learned that food brought everyone together regardless of religion, political views, salaries, or social status. It was a common ground that most people were open to discussing freely – the best thing they've eaten, what grandma or grandpa makes, the history of certain dishes.

This book is not only your passport to seeing the world using food as a compass, it's a diary of experiences and conversations that I have had with locals in different countries. Travel opened my eyes and showed me how small we are compared to the world beyond us and I hope this book gives you a glimpse into our beautiful world!

A traditional turbaned man in Rajasthan, India

The Merlion statue in Singapore symbolizes cultural values locals possess including courage, bravery, and a forward thinking attitude through it's lion head. The mermaid body represents the hard-working, thrifty, and down to earth nature inherent in the aura of the city due to its beginnings as a fishing village.

ACKNOWLEDGEMENTS

This book would not have been possible without the efforts put forth by many. I am especially indebted to my Mother who supported my vision throughout the making of this book.

I am grateful to all of those with whom I have had the pleasure to meet and work with during my journey of creating this book. I would especially like to thank the following individuals for their contributions:

- Ashlee Knapp; Thank you for giving me the title of this book.

- Jessika Roth, my editor; Thank you for making my words flow.

- Bob Levine, layout; Thank you for bringing all of the pieces together to create a beautiful final product.

- Inkquisitive Illustrations; Thank you for the exquisite cover art!

- Caitlin McCauley; Thank you for the graphic design in order to incorporate the cover art with my color inspiration to create the final cover.

- Muharrem Orhan; Thank you for coordinating all of my interactions in Turkey.

- Devendra Singh; Thank you for coordinating all photography efforts in India and Singapore.

- Carlos Salar; Thank you for the beautiful images from Spain.

- Badder Manaouch; Thank you for all of the Moroccan pictures.

- Jessika Roth; Thank you for the Pastel de Nata photo from Lisbon, Portugal.

- Natalie Symonds; Thank you for the lovely photos from New Zealand.

- Rajiv Bhuttan; Thank you for the lovely picture of the Istanbul skyline London's Underground.

- Rajinder P Jaggi & Raghav Jaggi; Thank you for sharing the recipe and story of the famed Butter Chicken with me. It is truly special to be able to include the story and details of this phenomena!

- ALX Creatives; Thank you for coordinating all of my headshots and photos of recipes that I personally made to photograph for this book. Thank you to Benny Cuppini for being a patient and collaborative photographer.

- Zoe Apostolidou; Thank you for the beautiful pictures from London's Borough Market and various other places in Europe.

- Chef Joaquim Saragga Leal; Thank you for allowing me in your restaurant kitchen and sharing some of your secret recipes with me.

- Grgo Gunjaca; Thank you for being so in love with Croatia and wanting to share it with me.

Thank you to all other photographers and hundreds of people that I have met throughout the world along this journey.

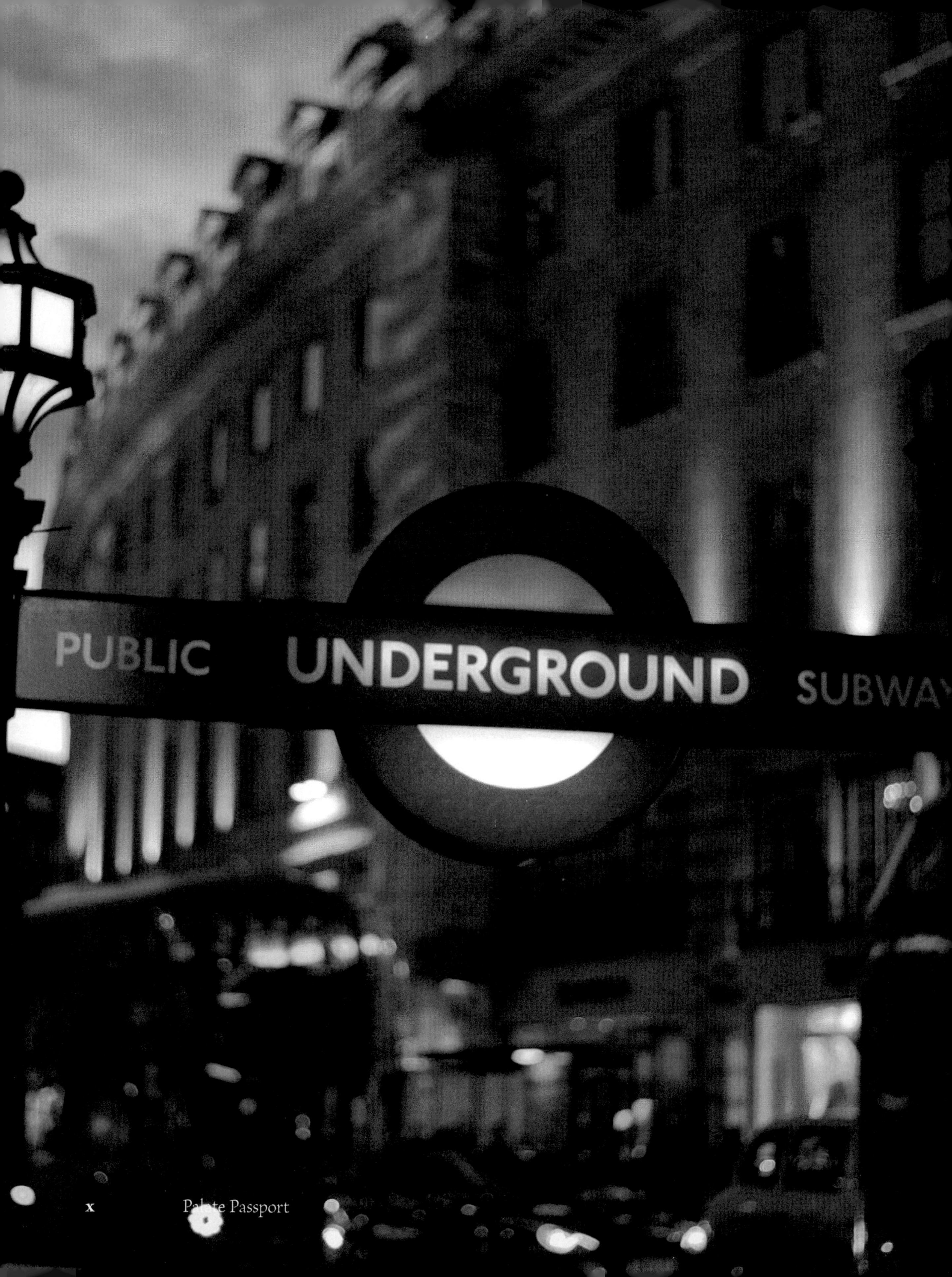
PUBLIC
UNDERGROUND
SUBWAY

CONTENTS

Palate Passport

"A woman named Piri"
Artist unknown,
Capetown, South Africa

SAUCES

Ajvar

5 medium red bell peppers

1 medium eggplant

5 medium garlic cloves – minced

1 tablespoon white vinegar

1 teaspoon salt, plus more to taste

¼ cup olive oil

Freshly ground black pepper to taste

1. Preheat oven to 375 degrees.

2. In a large bowl, drizzle 1 teaspoon of olive oil over the peppers and mix until well-coated.

3. Pour the peppers and eggplant onto a foil-lined baking pan. Bake for about 1 hour.

4. Remove the peppers from the oven when they are blackened all over. Place them in a bowl, cover with plastic wrap and steam for about 20 minutes. Remove the charred skin, seeds, and core of the peppers and discard.

5. Remove the eggplant from the oven when it is completely charred. Let it sit for 10 minutes or until completely cooled. Trim off the top of the eggplant and cut lengthwise. Using a spoon, scoop out the flesh of the eggplant and discard the skin.

6. Place the roasted red peppers, eggplant pulp, and garlic in a food processor; pulse until roughly chopped. Add the rest of the olive oil, vinegar, and salt; pulse until the mixture is smooth.

7. Transfer the sauce to a medium saucepan and bring to a simmer over medium-high heat. Reduce the heat to medium-low and simmer for 30 minutes, stirring occasionally.

8. Remove from heat and season with salt and pepper to taste.

9. Let the sauce cool to room temperature. Use immediately or transfer to an airtight container to store in the refrigerator for up to 2 weeks.

This sauce is a must for a Ćevapčići sandwich (p. 128) and can also be used as a dip or cheeseboard accompaniment.

Traditional outdoor cooking in the mountains of Split, Croatia

The recipe for Ajvar, or *Serbian Salsa* as it's also called, differs from home to home across the Balkan Region. The addition of chili peppers, different types of oils, and varying amounts of eggplant are all variations that make each recipe unique. Ajvar is considered *Zimnica*, a Serbian term referring to foods that are pickled and jarred right before winter such as pickled chili peppers and pickled tomatoes. It's a savory roasted red pepper and eggplant dish that is ritually made close to fall during peak harvest time for red peppers.

The bright red peppers are bought in bulk and then roasted over an open fire. Making Ajvar can be an all-day affair when families and friends gather together to make batch after batch to last the entire winter. Once the peppers are roasted, they are cooled, peeled, ground with any other desired ingredients, and jarred.

The smoky and tangy spread, which features red peppers, eggplant, minced garlic, olive oil, and vinegar, can be used as a bright garnish for grilled meats, paired with Mediterranean salads for a mezze platter, or simply devoured on a piece of crusty bread drizzled with olive oil.

I tasted Ajvar for the first time after a night out in Diocletian's Palace in Split. A popular late-night nosh on the streets of Croatia is Ćevapčići (p. 128)—a Croatian sausage rolled in flatbread and topped with a lot of Ajvar and chopped onions. The moment I bit into the Ćevapčići flatbread, I was instantly loving the slightly seasoned, greasy meat but what really stood out was the addition of the smoky, sweet and salty Ajvar. It added a certain warmth and even a level of elegance to the 2 a.m. calorie gorge. The flavor immediately caught my attention since US late-night eats don't typically include a roasted red pepper dip; it's usually something one would see on a menu for gourmet sandwiches. In Croatia, even a late-night snack is treated with respect for one's palate!

SPICY FETA DIP

1 cup feta cheese

¾ cup roasted red peppers–peeled, seeded, and chopped

5 pepperoncini peppers–stemmed and seeded

1 teaspoon cayenne pepper

1 cup ricotta cheese

2 tablespoons pepperoncini juice

1 teaspoon lemon juice

1. Place the feta in a food processor and pulse until fine crumbles are formed. Transfer them to a medium bowl.

2. Puree the red peppers, pepperoncini, pepperoncini juice, and cayenne pepper in the food processor until smooth. Place the mixture in the same bowl as the feta.

3. Add the ricotta cheese and lemon juice to the bowl. Mix everything together until the entire dip has an even texture and color.

4. Put the dip in a sealed container and refrigerate for at least 2 hours (and up to overnight) before serving.

I absolutely love this dip. I had it for the first time at a tiny, family-owned Greek eatery in New York City. I was picking up my order of Souvlaki Salad and walked past an orange dip with a sticker that said "Spicy Feta Dip". I like spicy. I like feta. I love dipping my extra pita in something. I thought why not, picked up a container, and asked about it.

The entire family's eyes lit up when I asked what it was. They said, "You will love it!" And love it I did! The saltiness from the feta, creaminess from the ricotta, pickled spiciness from the pepperoncini, and smoky sweetness from the red pepper came together perfectly in this dip.

Although I haven't been to Greece to taste the dip there, I received this recipe from a Greek grandmother that I met at London's Heathrow Airport during a layover–it was just meant to be included in this book!

I usually serve Spicy Feta Dip with pita or sliced cucumbers. Warning–it's addicting!

FAVA BEAN DIP

2 cups cooked fava beans*

2 garlic cloves – pressed

½ teaspoon white
wine vinegar

⅛ teaspoon sea salt

¼ cup extra virgin olive oil

Juice of one lemon

Optional garnishes

Smoked paprika

Best quality olive oil

Parsley – chopped

*Canned fava beans work here, but if
they are difficult to find, purchase the
dried beans and cook per instructions.*

Facade of a house in Athens, Greece

1. Place the cooked beans, garlic, salt, lemon juice, and vinegar in a food processor; pulse until well-combined.

2. Continue to pulse the machine as you slowly drizzle the olive oil through the lid opening; process until smooth.

3. Transfer the mixture to a serving bowl and garnish as desired. Serve this dip with crusty bread or pita chips.

The first time I had fava bean dip was in Turkey. After filling myself with hummus as an accompaniment to every meal, a Turkish friend recommended that I try this dip for a change. Its simplicity, creaminess, and distinct flavor drawn from the use of fava beans rather than garbanzo beans got me hooked. People in Turkey and Greece make this dip to eat with pita, raw vegetables, and vegetable fritters. This creamy dip goes perfectly with my salty and crunchy Zucchini Feta Fritters (p. 205)!

Coconut trees in the
backwaters of Kerala, India

SOUTH INDIAN TOMATO CHUTNEY

2 medium onions – chopped

3 Roma tomatoes – chopped

1 tablespoon dried split bengal gram

1-2 dried red chilis

1 teaspoon mustard seeds

1 teaspoon cumin

6-7 curry leaves

½ teaspoon tamarind pulp

1 tablespoon roasted coconut

1 tablespoon olive oil

Pinch of asafoetida or hing*

Salt to taste

Asafoetida is an herb native to Persia and India, and is readily available in South Asian grocery stores. Omit completely if it cannot be found.

1. In a non-stick pan on low heat, add olive oil, split bengal gram, red chilis, mustard seeds, cumin, coconut, and curry leaves. Cook for 1 minute.

2. Add the onions and sauté until they turn light brown.

3. Add the tomatoes, asafoetida, and salt to taste. Sauté until the tomatoes become soft and pulpy.

4. Allow the mixture to cool. When cool, add it to a blender with the tamarind pulp.

5. Puree the mixture and add more salt if desired.

Breakfast in India is special. In homes throughout the country, an authentic breakfast is typically savory rather than sweet, and is hearty to ensure a proper start to your day. It usually includes a type of buttery, wheat-based flatbread or a fermented rice-based dish along with eggs, potatoes, or a lentil soup, varying based on which state you're in. Condiments and pickles are a must with every meal in order to satisfy the Indian palate of sweet, spicy, crunchy, creamy, and salty all in one bite. Meals are a feast, even breakfast!

Whenever I stay at a hotel in India, I always fill up on breakfast – first because I've never been sick from food at a luxury hotel in India and second, because I'm able to enjoy western foods such as omelettes or scrambled eggs with Indian condiments. When I stayed at the ITC Grand Maratha in Mumbai, I did just that! I had a western omelette with a side of sausage, grilled mushrooms, and toast along with bowls full of different condiments to try.

As soon as I dipped my eggs into tomato chutney, my world changed. The sweetness from the tomato mixed with tart tamarind,

spicy red chilis, creamy coconut, and the distinct flavor of curry leaf did a dance on my tongue! I asked the waiter if I could speak with the chef and out came Executive Chef Sridhar Patra. After telling him how much I loved the chutney I asked for the recipe and he happily wrote it out for me.

When I make it nowadays, I store it in my refrigerator for up to 1 week. I use it with my eggs or even as a dip for potato chips!

PICCALILLI SAUCE

2 pounds mixed vegetables including: green beans, cucumbers, zucchinis, shallots or small onions, cauliflower, carrots, etc.

3 cups apple cider vinegar

¾ cup sugar

2 teaspoons ground turmeric

2 tablespoons fresh ginger root–grated

3 teaspoons mustard seeds

1 teaspoon cumin seeds

1 teaspoon coriander seeds

2 ounces cornflour

2 teaspoons English mustard powder

Salt to taste

1. Roughly chop all of the vegetables. Place them in a colander and rinse.

2. Sprinkle the vegetables with a decent amount of salt and leave them covered in a dark place for about 24 hours.

3. In a large saucepan, bring the vinegar and sugar to a boil, then reduce the heat to a simmer.

4. Crush the turmeric, ginger, mustard seeds, cumin seeds, and coriander seeds using a mortar and pestle. Add the cornflour, mustard powder and about a teaspoon of the heated vinegar; mix to form a paste.

5. Add the paste to the simmering vinegar and continue to cook for 5 minutes. Remove the pan from the heat.

6. Add all of the vegetables to the saucepan and mix to coat with the pickling sauce.

7. Let the mixture cool. When completely cool, scoop into sterilized jars.

Use Piccalilli Sauce on sandwiches, with pretzels, or as part of your cheese platter. This sauce usually lasts in the refrigerator for about 1 week.

Cheeses at Borough Market in London, UK

During the 200 years of British rule over India, many traditions and foods between the two countries became intermingled. So much so that today Britain's national dish isn't a British dish at all, it's Chicken Tikka Masala, a spin-off of a staple in Indian cuisine–chopped tandoori chicken drenched in a creamy, slightly sweet and spicy tomato sauce. The original Chicken Tikka is spice-rubbed chicken cooked in a clay oven, a prized possession of northern India, hailing from the state of Punjab. The British added the spiced gravy to satisfy their tradition of serving meat with gravy for Sunday supper.

Britain's interest in Indian cooking didn't stop there. They were influenced by India's affinity for pickling using distinct spices. India has a variety of pickles called *Achars*: pickled lemons, mangoes, carrots, turnips, apples, or any other fruit or vegetable that you can imagine. These closely-guarded family recipes are passed down through generations of grandmothers, each having their own secret ingredient. Women in India from villages and cities alike spend hours on their terraces chopping ingredients, drying them for days to eliminate moisture, creating the perfect spice blend, and then finally cooking and bottling the resulting pickles. Certain families even make pickled minced meats!

The British brought this pickling method home, added a few of

Charcuterie cones at Borough Market in London, UK

their own ingredients and came up with Piccalilli Sauce. The first mention of Piccalilli Sauce can be found in 18th century British cookbooks which reference Indian pickles.

Piccalilli's distinctive yellow hue comes from the addition of turmeric. English mustard powder gives it a kick and also contributes to its bright color. The chunkier versions of the sauce are commonly used as an accompaniment to foods such as sausage, eggs, cheese, or as a relish in a cold-cut sandwich like ham and cheese.

Having grown up close to Philadelphia, a popular place for soft pretzels, I grew accustomed to eating Piccalilli Sauce on doughy, warm pretzels. These days I use it as a dip for my Pretzel Crusted Calamari (p. 159).

Doña Sauce

1 pound jalapeños

6 garlic cloves – unpeeled

1 tablespoon apple
cider vinegar

¼ teaspoon salt

¼ cup vegetable oil

1. Preheat oven to 375 degrees.

2. In a bowl, drizzle 1 teaspoon of oil onto the peppers and mix.

3. Pour the peppers onto a foil-lined baking pan and bake until all sides have browned.

4. Transfer the peppers to a bowl and cover with plastic wrap to steam.

5. Next, roast the garlic cloves under the broiler until all sides have browned.

6. When cool, peel the skin from the garlic and peppers. Seed and devein the peppers, then discard the skin, seeds and veins.

7. Place the peppers and garlic in a blender. Add the vinegar and salt and puree.

8. Slowly add the oil until a smooth, creamy texture is achieved.

9. Place in an airtight bottle and refrigerate.

The possibilities are endless with this sauce! Use it as a topping on tacos, nachos, burgers… just about anything, really.

"Keep Austin Weird" is the official city slogan.

Many parts of the world have a version of green sauce to spruce up the flavor quotient in their dishes including Brazilian Chimichurri, Moroccan Chermoula, Italian Pesto, and Indian Mint Chutney, to name a few.

Tacodeli, a taco shop in Austin, Texas serves a green sauce called Doña Sauce, which locals refer to as *Green Crack*. It's smooth, velvety, and spicy with an initially pleasing burn that encourages topping each bite of soft taco with more and more sauce until you just can't take any more!

Doña Sauce's origin dates back to around the time Tacodeli opened and a beautiful Mexican woman was hired to work in their kitchen. Long before working there, she had run her own taco truck in Veracruz, Mexico, where she made a fiery green sauce from roasted jalapeños. She was quickly referred to as Doña, a term used to show respect and admiration for a powerful woman. The owners held a salsa contest with their customers as judges, Doña entered her green salsa recipe, it won, claiming a permanent place on the menu–and the rest is history!

Locals and visitors alike have been known to flock to Austin's Tacodeli chain just for the famed Doña sauce. Every day, each location roasts around 60 pounds of jalapeños to make enough sauce to meet customer demands.

After hearing about the *Green Crack* from friends, I obviously had to taste it. After falling in love with it myself, I tried to get the recipe, but learned it remains a closely-guarded secret. I decided if I couldn't have their recipe, I'd make my own. I went back and tasted the sauce a few times to really get a feel for its flavors, tested a few batches of the sauce, and eventually pulled it off. I have to say–I'm addicted to this version!

Colorful beach houses of Muizenberg Beach,
a suburb of Capetown, South Africa

SOUTH AFRICAN PERI PERI SAUCE

½ onion – chopped

½ red bell pepper

3-4 jalapeños

2 medium hot red chili peppers*

1 tablespoon smoked paprika

1 tablespoon tomato paste

6-7 garlic cloves

1 teaspoon coconut or palm sugar

1 tablespoon vinegar

2 teaspoons oregano

2 teaspoons salt, adjust to taste

1 cup olive oil

Juice of one lemon

*Bird's eye chili is the authentic red chili pepper used in the recipe. It can be found in grocery stores or in Asian markets, otherwise any other red chili pepper will work.

1. Blend all of the ingredients in a food processor or blender to make the sauce/marinade.

Peri Peri or *Piri Piri* is Swahili for "Pepper Pepper". Variations of the sauce have been around since the 15th century when Portuguese settlers in Africa came across the African bird's eye chili, which grows wild in countries such as South Africa, Zimbabwe, and Nigeria. They made a marinade with it by adding garlic, vinegar, paprika, and other European imports. Today a popular UK chain called Nando's hangs its hat on selling this tasty sauce.

When I went to South Africa to visit a friend native to the area, I obviously asked about the local delicacies. A dish called Peri Peri Chicken was the number one recommendation and did not fail to impress!

Peri Peri wasn't a hot sauce or a barbecue sauce, and it certainly did not appear to have Asian flavors like a soy sauce, yet the taste had qualities that could be compared to all three sauces. I was inspired by the sauce and developed this recipe which I now use on pork, lamb, and even on top of potatoes.

Traditional Braai in South Africa where Peri Peri sauce is used to flavor the meats. Braai is a social gathering to the South Africans. A specific outdoor grill is built and family and friends gather for an entire day of fun.

"Zween"–Artist: C.E.G., Marrakech, Morocco

SOUPS AND SALADS

Mexican Esquites

3 cups frozen corn kernels – defrosted

1 avocado – peeled, pitted, and diced

½ cup whole milk

2 ounces feta or Cotija cheese – finely crumbled

½ cup green scallions – chopped

½ cup fresh cilantro – chopped

1 jalapeño – finely chopped (remove the seeds for less heat)

2 garlic cloves – minced

1 tablespoon fresh lime juice

2 tablespoons vegetable oil

Chili powder or hot chili flakes to taste

Salt to taste

1. In a large non-stick pan on high heat, add the oil and corn; stir lightly.

2. Let the corn char slightly on one side before stirring to char the same amount on the other side. The idea is to get the street cart style grilled corn flavor through this process. Once charred, transfer the corn to a large bowl.

3. In a blender, add the avocado, milk, lime juice, and garlic; blend until a smooth paste forms.

4. Scoop the paste into the bowl with the corn and add cheese, chili powder, scallions, jalapeño, cilantro, and salt to taste. Serve immediately!

This is an authentic recipe from Mexico City resembling a popular street food called Elote – whole grilled corn on the cob slathered with all these yummy ingredients. Esquites, typically served in a cup, is a more dignified way to eat the same concept. My favorite way to enjoy this corn is with a beer or some other fizzy drink in hand!

QUICK JAPANESE TUNA SASHIMI SALAD

6 ounces sushi-grade tuna

1 apple – cored and chopped

1 avocado – pitted
and chopped

½ small red onion – finely
minced

1 tablespoon soy sauce

1 teaspoon Japanese
togarashi spice

1. Combine all of the ingredients and serve immediately with plantain or taro chips.

This is one of my favorite healthy yet flavorful dishes with the exotic twist of using Japanese togarashi spice. *Shichimi togarashi*, as it is authentically referred to, is a common Japanese spice blend containing seven ingredients: red chili pepper, ground roasted orange peel, black sesame seed, white sesame seed, ground ginger, nori (seaweed), and poppy seed. Some versions may include ground sanshō, a Japanese pepper similar to black pepper.

The origins of togarashi date back to 17th century apothecaries when red chilis were introduced to Japan as a form of medicine. In Asian cultures, herbs and spices were commingled with both food and medicine in the early days. This is something that I've seen first hand growing up in an Indian American household.

Togarashi has a fleeting, intense spiciness that fades as quickly as it comes, followed by a burst of sweetness and tanginess from the orange peel. In Japan, it is popularly eaten sprinkled on top of rice or noodle dishes, but my favorite way to indulge in this spice is by pairing it with non-traditional ingredients like I've done in this recipe.

CHICKEN TORTILLA SOUP

1 cup yellow onions – diced

1 large jalapeño – minced

4 garlic cloves – peeled and finely minced

32 ounces low-sodium chicken broth

2 (14.5-ounce) cans diced tomatoes

2 cups shredded cooked chicken*

1 ½ cups corn kernels

2 tablespoons lime juice

1 tablespoon chili powder

2 teaspoons cumin

1 teaspoon black pepper

1 teaspoon smoked paprika (regular paprika may be substituted)

¼ teaspoon cayenne pepper (optional)

⅓ cup fresh cilantro leaves – finely minced

2 teaspoons salt, adjust to taste

2 tablespoons olive oil

Optional garnishes

Tortilla chips – store-bought and crushed

Avocado – diced

Shredded cheese

Sour cream

Use store-bought rotisserie chicken to save time or cook your own chicken in a skillet.

1. Warm 2 tablespoons of olive oil in a large pot over medium-high heat.

2. Add the onion and jalapeño. Sauté for about 5 minutes, or until the vegetables begin to soften.

3. Add the garlic and sauté for another 1-2 minutes.

4. Add the chicken broth, tomatoes and juice, chicken, corn, lime juice, chili powder, cumin, 2 teaspoons of salt, pepper, smoked paprika, optional cayenne pepper, and bring to a boil. Allow the mixture to boil gently for about 5 minutes.

5. If you prefer your soup to have more broth, add 1-2 cups of water and boil; you'll adjust the salt and seasoning levels at the end.

6. Add the cilantro and boil 1 minute longer.

7. Taste the soup and add salt as needed. Make any necessary seasoning adjustments (i.e., more salt, pepper, chili powder, cumin, cayenne, etc.).

8. Ladle soup into bowls, top with tortilla strips to taste, and optionally garnish with avocado, cheese, and/or sour cream. Serve immediately.

A beautiful beach in Cancun, Mexico

Siblings–they are your best friends growing up, they steal your best clothes, fight with you about everything, tattle on you to elders, yet are willing to rip someone else's eyes out if they talk about you. My sister and I have had our fair share of experiences. We lived together in New Delhi, India at our grandparents home for a year when we were toddlers. We worked together at my parent's retail shop on the Jersey Shore until going to college. We made fake permission slips together in high school to ditch school and go see... wait for it... boys. After college, careers, life events, etc. we made time to travel together. We went to Toronto, Las Vegas, Rajasthan, India and eventually decided to go to Cancun for a party weekend in paradise.

We heard so much about the beaches, the music, the party scene, the vibe. Finally we booked a trip to go and stay at a 5-star, all-inclusive resort. Beachwear packed, sunglasses on, we cruised through the airport towards our flight, started our vacation with a Bloody Mary each, and soon enough we were hovering over Cancun. Since we went in November when it was quite cold in New York, we were instantly in awe of the sun's rays beaming onto the glittery turquoise ocean.

Then we landed–I sneezed, my sister coughed. Got our baggage–I coughed, my sister sneezed. We found our hotel transfer and my throat started to feel scratchy, congested, and my ears hurt when I swallowed. My sister felt her asthma attacks in small spurts. We were sick. Not just your run-of-the-mill sniffles and cough. This was a fever, fatigue, can't eat or swallow anything sick. My sister simply couldn't breathe–just minor things, you know. It was our first time to Mexico and the sickest we had felt in a decade!

So there we were in paradise for 5 days, with beautiful beaches surrounding us, tequila galore, party central and what did we do? We stayed in our hotel room and ordered room service which consisted of Chicken Tortilla Soup and coconut water–3 times a day, almost every day. It was the first time I had delicious, tangy and slightly spicy Chicken Tortilla Soup and I had lots of it!

What I'm trying to say is that the highlight of my first trip to Cancun was soup with hints of balcony sun and coconuts. And so I present you with my version of this memorable Chicken Tortilla Soup!

MALAYSIAN ACHAAT

1 large cucumber – cut lengthwise with the skin and seeds

¼ head of cabbage – cut into big pieces

1 large carrot – peeled and cut lengthwise

1 cup French beans – cut into 1 ½ inch pieces

½ cup roasted peanuts – ground

1 tablespoon sesame seeds

3 tablespoons olive oil

Sugar to taste

Salt to taste

For the spice paste

5 shallots

12 fresh red chilis

1 tablespoon turmeric powder

2 candlenuts or walnuts

For the tamarind juice*

¼ cup tamarind pulp (about golf ball size)

1 cup water

Store-bought tamarind juice can be used for this as well. If using, skip step 1 of the cooking process.

1. Soak the tamarind pulp in water for 15 minutes. Squeeze to extract the juice and set aside.

2. Blend the spice paste ingredients in a food processor and set aside.

3. Place a wok on medium heat, add oil, and stir-fry the spice paste until aromatic.

4. Add the tamarind juice and bring to a boil. Add salt and sugar to taste.

5. Add all of the vegetables and turn off the heat immediately.

6. Add the ground peanuts and sesame seeds; stir to mix well.

7. Let the mixture cool to room temperature and then serve or refrigerate if you'd like.

Achaat is a popular pickled vegetable from Malaysia that can be eaten as a condiment, or if you like it as much as I do, you'll eat it as a side salad. It's infused with an aromatic spice paste and finished with toasted ground peanuts and sesame seeds. It's so appetizing and addictive that it can be enjoyed with most Asian dishes like grilled fish, fried rice, or satay. I personally like to refrigerate the Achaat and then serve it cool with something grilled at a barbecue!

CAULIFLOWER SHOOTERS

2 cups cauliflower – chopped

4 cups vegetable stock

2 garlic cloves – peeled and sliced in half

½ cup shallots – peeled and roughly cut

2 tablespoons chives – chopped

2 tablespoons heavy cream

1 bottle truffle oil

1 tablespoon olive oil

Salt and pepper to taste

1. In a large saucepan on medium heat, add the olive oil, shallots and garlic; sauté for 3-4 minutes.

2. Add the cauliflower and sauté until the cauliflower is slightly soft, about 10 minutes.

3. Add the vegetable stock and bring to a boil.

4. Using a hand blender, blend the cauliflower into a soup-like puree. Add salt and pepper to taste.

5. Pour the cauliflower puree into shot glasses, top each glass with a drop of heavy cream, a pinch of chives, and a drop of truffle oil.

This soup shooter was inspired by a tiny amuse-bouche that I enjoyed before a beautiful French meal on the French side of St. Martin. It was a simply presented sip of creamy soup that started my meal off the right way – with something delicious. I've served this as an amuse-bouche, but have also eaten a full bowl of this soup on a cold winter night. Serve these shooters to your dinner guests to get them grinning before a fabulous meal!

Moroccan Harira Soup

2 onions – finely chopped

2 cups dried brown or red lentils

1 (14-ounce) can chickpeas

1 cup celery – finely chopped

3 tablespoons vegetable oil

1 teaspoon butter

½ teaspoon turmeric powder

4 garlic cloves – finely minced

1 cup parsley – chopped

1 cup cilantro – chopped

6 cups water

1 (12-ounce) can tomato sauce

2 tablespoons tomato paste

½ teaspoon black pepper

½ teaspoon ground ginger

½ cup vermicelli – broken into 1-inch pieces

½ cup all-purpose flour

3 tablespoons water – to mix with the flour

2 lemons – cut into wedges for serving

1 teaspoon salt

3 tablespoons olive oil

1. In a large saucepan on medium heat, add vegetable oil and butter and let the butter melt completely.

2. Add the chopped onions and celery and stir until the onions are translucent. Add the garlic and stir until slightly brown.

3. Add the parsley, cilantro, salt, and turmeric and mix for 3-5 minutes.

4. Add the lentils and water and boil for 1 hour, until the lentils are tender.

5. Add the chickpeas, tomato sauce, tomato paste, olive oil, ground ginger, and black pepper and boil for another 30 minutes.

6. Add the vermicelli to the soup, cover and cook on medium heat until the ver-micelli have cooked, about 5 minutes.

7. Mix the flour with enough water to form a smooth paste and add it to the soup to thicken it. Cook for 5 minutes or longer until the soup has thickened. Taste and adjust for seasoning. Serve hot with lemon wedges.

Harira in Marrakech, Morocco

Filled with lentils, vermicelli noodles or rice to thicken the mixture, as well as chickpeas and a blend of fresh herbs and spices, Harira is the national soup of Morocco. It's a staple everyday food and also traditionally eaten during the month of Ramadan. At sunset to break the day's fast, the tomato-based soup is served with a side of dates and honey-soaked sweet pastries.

A local restaurant owner in Marrakech explained to me that during winter months small street-side cafes set up stalls to serve warming bowls of Harira with a cup of mint tea and a pastry to locals making their way home from work in the late afternoon. It almost becomes an affordable ritual for the working class of the city to gather for a bowl of this soup. As soon as I heard this, I immediately thought of happy hours in New York that I would regularly enjoy with colleagues on my way home from work.

Once prepared, Harira is served piping hot in a bowl, and unlike other Moroccan dishes that are consumed with one's hands, a wooden spoon is traditionally used to slurp up the soup. These wooden spoons are sold throughout the windy medina streets in Marrakech. The soup is usually served with crusty bread for dipping and locals add a squeeze of lemon for a bit of zest. Every time I had the soup in Morocco, I didn't receive a wooden spoon to slurp with, but I always added a squeeze of lemon!

This was my personal comfort food while in Morocco. It was actually the first thing that I ate when I arrived in Marrakech with friends. The familiarity of having a piping hot lentil soup, with the new exotic flavors, had me coming back for a bowl of this soup almost every day! I received this particular recipe from a small street stall in Jamaa el Fna market in Marrakech during an afternoon when I took a stroll to see what the street food scene is like in the city. I hope you enjoy this recipe and savor this soup during the winter months!

Portuguese Caldo Verde

10 Idaho potatoes – peeled and roughly cut

2 white onions – chopped

2 garlic cloves

1 large bay leaf

½ teaspoon pepper

1 cup linguiça, chouriço, or sausage of your choice (optional)

5 cups kale – shredded

5 cups chicken stock

5 cups water

1 tablespoon salt

¼ cup olive oil

1. In a large stockpot on medium heat, add in olive oil, onions, and garlic; sauté until the onions are translucent.

2. Add in the potatoes, bay leaf, salt, and pepper; sauté until the potatoes are slightly soft.

3. Pour in the chicken stock and water. Boil until the potatoes are cooked through – you should be able to pierce a fork through the potato completely.

4. Remove the pot from the heat, remove the bay leaf, and blend the contents using a hand blender.

5. Place the pot back on low heat and continue to simmer the soup for 20 minutes.

6. If using linguiça or sausage, add it at this point and boil with the soup until completely cooked.

7. Taste for seasoning and add more salt or pepper if needed.

8. To serve, place the shredded kale in each serving bowl and ladle the soup into each bowl. Serve immediately as you do not want the kale to wilt before serving.

Viana do Castelo in what was a former province of Minho, Portugal

Caldo Verde is a pillar of Portuguese cuisine and praised as one of the "Seven Wonders of Portuguese Gastronomy," as voted by the Portuguese people. It is a fairly simple dish with potatoes, kale, olive oil, and salt as your canvas before adding other ingredients you wish to include. Traditionally, sliced choriço or linguiça is added for a meaty flavor, but it is not required if you wish to keep this soup vegetarian.

Hailing from Minho, the northern region of Portugal, it is thought that this soup was inspired by the Celtic's use of cabbage from their rule in Portugal which began in the first millennium BC. Over time, locals began adding different ingredients. The recipe changed based on locally available greens, mainly kale, and with the introduction of pork sausages to the soup such as the chouriço brought from the Roman Empire. This soup became an entire meal in some households. It is invariably served at celebrations throughout the country and beyond those days, may be savored at the start of a meal or as the meal itself.

I ate this soup the first night that I arrived in Lisbon. I fell in love with the creaminess from the potatoes, the vibrant green kale, and the slightly salty, meaty flavor from the chouriço medallion. I was also impressed by the overall healthy feeling this soup provides given the proportion of green, leafy kale. There is no doubt that Caldo Verde is a staple in Portuguese homes and a must-try for anyone seeking a taste of Portugal!

TAMARIND HEARTS OF PALM SALAD

1 cup hearts of palm

1 cup carrots

1 cup snow peas

1 teaspoon tamarind pulp

1 teaspoon black
sesame seeds

¼ cup toasted almond slices

½ teaspoon sea salt

1 tablespoon olive oil

1. Remove the stems from each side of the snow peas. Thinly slice the snow peas into vertical strips and place in a medium-sized bowl.

2. Thinly slice the hearts of palm into noodle-like strips and add to the snow peas.

3. Using a julienne cutter, cut the carrots into noodle-like strips and add to the mixture.

4. In a separate bowl, mix together the tamarind pulp, oil, and sea salt.

5. Dress the slaw with the tamarind dressing and garnish with the sesame seeds and almonds.

This is a delicious and healthy salad inspired by Thailand with its tamarind flavors and by Belize with its use of hearts of palm. I had an interesting experience when I ordered this salad in Belize and the ingredients looked like noodles more than anything. After tasting it and asking about the main ingredient, I was told hearts of palm were thinly sliced to look like noodles. It was a eureka moment to discover using hearts of palm in this way. I hope you enjoy the textures and flavors of this salad as much as I do!

Farmhouse in the rainforest of Belize

FISH BALL SOUP

1 pound white fish (such as cod, haddock, or halibut)

4 tablespoons cold water

2 teaspoons cornflour

6 cups boiling water

1 cup glass noodles (Chinese vermicelli or cellophane noodles)

1 bunch bok choy

2 tablespoons soy sauce

2 cups chicken broth

3 spring onion sprigs – chopped

1 red Thai chili – seeded and sliced

1 thick slice of ginger

½ teaspoon salt

1 tablespoon sesame oil

Pinch of white pepper powder

Optional garnishes

Spring onions – chopped

Chilis – thinly sliced

1. Soak the glass noodles for 10 minutes in 1 ½ cups of boiling water; drain, rinse under cold water, drain again, and set aside.

2. Place the following ingredients into a food processor to make the fish balls: fish, cold water, cornflour, salt, and white pepper powder. Blend until it forms a smooth paste.

3. Remove the paste onto a lightly floured surface. Lift the paste and smack it down onto the work surface; repeat this 30-40 times. This should make the fish balls springy and light in texture.

4. Place in the refrigerator for 1 hour; remove, mold into bite-sized balls with your hands, and set aside.

5. Pour the remaining boiling water into a pot. Add the soy sauce, sesame oil, chicken stock, chili, ginger, and spring onions. Boil on medium heat for 2 minutes.

6. Gently drop in the fish balls and boil them for 5 minutes.

7. Wash the bok choy, cut into thick strips, and add into the pot, followed by adding in the noodles. Simmer on low heat for 2 minutes.

8. Ladle into bowls and scatter with garnishes if you wish.

This is a Chinese-inspired soup that is very popular in Thailand and a staple amongst foodies at hawker markets in Singapore. When I later saw fish balls in Iceland I learned that these ingredients are common for soups in Nordic countries as well. In the Nordic countries, the fish balls are made with milk and mostly cod or haddock; a very light steaming technique is used to cook them. The Chinese usually boil the fish balls but frying is also very popular. I've had this soup in China, Thailand, Singapore and in Iceland and the traditional Chinese version is by far my favorite. You can add your desired level of salt or spice using the soy sauce and peppers – it's divine!

ROASTED POBLANO AND CORN SOUP

4 poblano peppers – roasted, peeled, seeded, and chopped

1 cup yellow onions – diced

2 teaspoons garlic powder

2 teaspoons cumin

2 teaspoons chili powder

1 teaspoon oregano

4 garlic cloves – minced

6 cups chicken broth

3 cups frozen corn

3 tablespoons cornmeal mixed with a splash of water

8 ounces Monterey Jack cheese – shredded

1 cup sour cream

¼ teaspoon cayenne pepper

1 teaspoon salt

1 tablespoon olive oil

1. In a large pot over medium-high heat, add olive oil and sauté the onions and garlic until the onions begin to soften.

2. Add garlic powder, salt, cumin, chili powder, cayenne pepper and oregano; sauté for 1 minute.

3. Add the chicken broth, corn, and poblanos and bring the mixture to a boil.

4. Add the cornmeal mixture into the soup and stir well.

5. Reduce the heat to low and simmer the soup for 15-20 minutes. Allow the cornmeal to thicken the soup during this time.

6. Right before serving, add in the sour cream and cheese and stir until the cheese is completely melted on low heat.

This soup is inspired by Mexican flavors and one of my go-tos for entertaining! I hardly ever have leftovers whenever I make this. Spoon it into bowls and serve with sliced avocado, more cheese, cilantro, pickled onions, and/or tortilla chips… take your pick!

CUCUMBER POMEGRANATE SALAD

2 cups cucumbers – diced

½ cup pomegranate seeds

¼ cup cilantro

½ cup crumbled feta

1 tablespoon lemon juice

Salt and pepper to taste

1. In a large bowl, mix all of the ingredients except for feta. Season with salt and pepper to taste.

2. Divide the salad among bowls and top with feta.

This salad has creamy cheese, sweet and tart pomegranate, cool cucumbers, and a simple lemon and salt dressing to bring it all together. Inspired by my travels in the Middle Eastern and Mediterranean regions, this salad is summer in a bowl!

ISRAELI BEETS WITH TEHINA

12-15 garlic cloves

1 cup sesame tahini paste

1 teaspoon ground cumin

6 beets – halved

¾ cup lemon juice

1 tablespoon fresh dill

¼ cup fresh parsley,
plus more for topping

1 tablespoon salt

½ cup oil

1. Preheat oven to 375 degrees. Place parchment paper at the bottom of a baking pan, drizzle with a little oil, and sprinkle a pinch of salt.

2. Place the beets on the parchment paper and sprinkle with 2 teaspoons of salt to give the beets a nice coating. Bake on the medium rack of the oven for 1 ½ hours.

3. While the beets are baking, make the tehina. In a blender, pulse the garlic and ½ cup of the lemon juice until a puree is formed.

4. In a medium-sized mixing bowl, add cumin and tahini paste to the lemon garlic liquid and combine with a whisk.

5. Add water little by little while continuing to whisk until a smooth sauce is formed. Season with salt to taste and set aside.

6. Once the beets are completely tender, remove them from the oven and let cool to room temperature.

7. Grate the beets using a box grater and add to the tehina. Mix in the remaining lemon juice, oil, dill, and parsley. Add salt to taste.

I transform a typical beet salad into a creamy, tart version so it can take the place of a usual pita-stuffer or stand up solo as a new salad variation. Spoon the beets into a beautiful serving bowl, garnish with more parsley or a drizzle of olive oil, and serve with kebabs, fresh crusty bread, or warm pita.

CRÈME DE TOMATE EN CROUTE

½ cup unsalted butter

½ pound yellow
onions – sliced

6 garlic cloves

1 bay leaf

½ tablespoon whole
black peppercorns

1 teaspoon dried
thyme leaves

¼ cup tomato paste

2 ½ pounds ripe
tomatoes – cored
and quartered

1 cup water (optional – use
only if the tomatoes
aren't ripe and juicy)

4 cups heavy cream

2-4 tablespoons butter

½ teaspoon ground
white pepper

1 pound puff pastry or
store-bought sheets

1 egg – beaten with 1
tablespoon water

Salt to taste

1. Melt the ½ cup of butter in a large stockpot over medium-low heat. Add the onions, garlic, thyme, bay leaf, and peppercorns; cover and cook for about 5 minutes. Do not let the onions color.

2. Add the tomato paste and lightly "toast" the tomato paste to remove the raw flavor. Add the tomatoes, and water if needed. Simmer over low heat for 30-40 minutes, until the tomatoes and onions are very soft and broken down.

3. Puree by passing through a food mill. A food mill works best, however you may use a blender in batches or a handheld immersion blender. Strain when finished blending and return the soup to the pot.

4. Add the cream, salt, white pepper, and remaining butter to taste. Bring the soup to a simmer then remove from heat. Allow the soup to cool for 2 hours or overnight in the refrigerator.

5. Divide the soup among six 8-ounce soup cups. Roll out the puff pastry to ¼ inch thick. Cut 6 round pieces slightly larger than your cups. Paint the dough with the egg wash and turn the circles, egg wash side down, over the tops of the cups, pulling lightly on the sides to make the dough somewhat tight like a drum. Try not to allow the dough to touch the soup. These may be made up to 24 hours in advance and covered with plastic in the refrigerator.

6. Preheat oven to 450 degrees.

7. Lightly paint the exposed tops of the dough rounds with egg wash without pushing the dough down. Bake for 10-15 minutes, until the dough is golden brown. Do not open the oven in the first several minutes of cooking as the dough may fall. Serve immediately.

Castello di Amorosa, Napa Valley, California

France–the country known for its use of butter. It seems as though every dish is competing with the other in its lush quotient. Why would tomato soup be any different? Only the French would know how to take a simple tomato soup and put it over the top in creaminess and presentation. I was certainly captured in its spell, enough to put it in this book!

I tasted crème de tomate, "creamy tomato soup," while in France, but didn't think much of it except that it was creamy and I would have to work it off with extra time at the gym. Years later a friend and I made one of our many trips to Napa and indulged in a local French eatery called Bistro Jeanty. We just had to have what everyone was ordering around us because it came out with an amazing presentation that one couldn't miss. Out came Crème de Tomate en Croute, and I was in heaven–it took me straight back to France. I hope you savor every bite just like I did!

MOROCCAN CARROT SALATIM

8 large carrots – peeled

1 garlic clove – minced

⅓ cup orange juice

2 tablespoons lemon juice

½ cup cilantro – chopped

1 tablespoon fresh
mint – chopped

½ teaspoon cayenne pepper

½ teaspoon paprika

1 teaspoon cumin powder

¼ cup olive oil

Sea salt

1. Place the carrots in a deep pan and add enough water to slightly cover the carrots.

2. Add a pinch of salt and cook the carrots on medium-high heat for about 10 minutes.

3. Remove the carrots with a slotted spoon and reserve the cooking liquid.

4. Simmer the cooking liquid on low until reduced and almost syrupy, about 10-15 minutes.

5. Add the garlic and cook for 2 more minutes.

6. Remove the pan from the heat and add the remaining ingredients including salt to taste, about 1 teaspoon; whisk it well to combine.

7. When the carrots are cool enough to handle, slice them into discs.

8. Toss the carrots into the liquid mixture and refrigerate the salad to chill it prior to serving.

A farmer celebrating a successful harvest of vegetables in Morocco

I was advised not to eat vegetables in Morocco due to a lack of water cleanliness. But I didn't care–after eating meat and bread for days, I was craving fresh vegetables. I decided I would eat them anyways and enjoyed every little bit of this crispy carrot salad.

Oranges are a common dessert in Morocco–just simple sliced oranges with a sprinkle of cinnamon are welcome after a heavy meal. It is so satisfying and perfect. I came to learn how orange essence and orange juice is a common addition to salads in Morocco.

I now embrace adding orange flavors with open arms and so should you! Enjoy this orange-flavored carrot salad with grilled meat or with a full Moroccan meal.

CORDOBA SALMOREJO

10 medium tomatoes (bright red Celebrity tomatoes work great)

1 medium baguette – crust removed

1 garlic clove

1 tablespoon sherry vinegar

2 hard-boiled eggs – diced

¾ cup serrano ham – chopped

1 teaspoon salt

1 cup extra virgin olive oil

1. Blanch the tomatoes by boiling a large pot of salted water and dropping the tomatoes in for 1 minute, then quickly removing the tomatoes and putting them in a cold water bath.

2. Peel the skin off the tomatoes (this should be easy now) and remove the core.

3. In a blender, add the tomatoes and blend until the tomatoes are broken down.

4. Cut up the baguette (there should be about 3 cups with crust removed) and add it to the blender. Let the bread soak in the tomato juice.

5. Add the sherry vinegar, salt, and garlic; blend until the bread is completely pureed.

6. Open the top notch of the blender and slowly drizzle in the olive oil while continuing to blend. If you do not have a top notch, then turn off the blender and add the olive oil in increments before continuing to blend.

7. Adjust the seasoning and ladle the soup into small serving bowls. Top the soup with the eggs and ham and enjoy!

Roman Bridge in Cordoba, Spain

Many people have heard of Gazpacho, the popular cold soup from Spain. However, not many people have heard of Salmorejo which is another popular cold soup that originated in Cordoba, Spain. Salmorejo requires just a few common, inexpensive ingredients and is easy to make so this is a great dish for a novice chef to make for a taste of Spanish gastronomy on a tight budget!

The history of Salmorejo has evolved over time with its roots dating back to the Roman Empire who used bread as an ingredient in sauces. Once Christopher Columbus brought tomatoes to the region from Latin America, the soup went from a blanco (white) version to a roja (red) one.

I first spotted Salmorejo while living in Valencia, Spain. For a month I lived about twenty steps from the Central Market, the hub of food activity in the city. Amazing ingredients are on display – various sorts of paprika, all kinds of meat and seafood, stalls filled with Jamon Serrano and Iberico, piles of Spanish cheeses, and of course, paella pans too. It was basically my playground for the month.

Along with Central Market, I would frequent the local supermarket chain called Mercadona to buy staple ingredients like milk, eggs, and juice and also to see what the Valencians use to make their weekly meals. That's where I saw cartons of Gazpacho and right next to it – cartons of Salmorejo. Locals who came to buy ingredients for dinner on their way home from work were picking up these ready-made cartons of soup. I followed along and also picked up the Salmorejo, then I headed toward the meat counter to get some ground chicken.

I asked the butcher about the Salmorejo. He looked at me, snickered a bit, and then explained in English that it is a cold soup that is thicker than Gazpacho due to the use of bread. While Gazpacho is served with a garnish of chopped vegetables, locals typically serve Salmorejo with chopped eggs and sliced serrano ham. However, restaurants get more creative with toppings such as crab meat.

Here I've shared my version of the traditional recipe. It's great to have on a hot summer afternoon!

Turkish Ezme

2 tomatoes – peeled

1 onion

1 garlic clove

2 jalapeños (or long hot peppers)

¼ bunch parsley

1 tablespoon lemon juice

2 tablespoons pomegranate molasses (or concentrated pomegranate juice)

1 teaspoon Turkish pepper paste (biber salcasi) or tomato paste mixed with chili powder

½ teaspoon chili powder

½ teaspoon sumac (or lemon zest mixed with a pinch of salt)

2 tablespoons olive oil

Pinch of dried mint

Salt to taste

1. Finely dice tomatoes, onions, jalapeños, parsley, and garlic and mix them in a large bowl.

2. In a separate bowl, mix together the lemon juice, pomegranate molasses, olive oil, and pepper paste until smooth.

3. Add the dressing to the salad along with all of the remaining spices and mix well. Add salt to taste.

4. Chill in the refrigerator for half an hour and serve cold. This step is very important as it helps the flavors fuse together.

Serve Turkish Ezme with hummus, with cheese and crackers, with kebabs, or with breakfast-style eggs. Be prepared for a dance in your mouth!

This tomato-based salad, or dip as some see it, is spicy and zingy yet crisp and refreshing all at the same time. It originates from southeastern Turkey where spicy food is quite prevalent. The full name of the dish is Antep Ezmesi, which is referred to as *Ezme* in short, a Turkish word that means "crushed".

In Turkey, you might see the term elsewhere such as in descriptions on restaurant menus. I was initially confused when I kept seeing "Ezme" everywhere and assumed it had to do with tomatoes! It is a very typical mezze, served in kebab houses all over Turkey as a side salad to eat with your meaty goodness.

When I visited Turkey, I ate Ezme with practically every meal. Every single serving tasted different as every chef added their own proportions of the same ingredients. To me, what makes this salad unique is the addition of pomegranate molasses for that sweet and distinct tangy flavor. It's the perfect accompaniment for a kebab platter or just to have with pita and hummus!

Spice dunes at the Egyptian Bazaar in Istanbul, Turkey.
Named the Egyptian Bazaar as the structure was built
from revenues that the Ottoman earned from Egypt, the
bazaar was once the center for spice trade in the world.

"Majestic Rang"–Artist: Pallab Baruah, New Delhi, India

CHICKEN AND EGGS

CHICKEN FARCHA

12 boneless chicken thighs

2 tablespoons red chili powder

1 teaspoon green chilis, or more to taste

1 teaspoon turmeric powder

1 tablespoon jeera powder

½ tablespoon ginger – finely minced

½ tablespoon garlic – finely minced

2 tablespoons cilantro leaves – finely chopped

4 egg whites – whisked until soft peaks form

½ cup semolina flour

3 tablespoons vegetable oil, for shallow frying

Juice of one lemon

Salt to taste

Parsis refer to this dish as Murghi na Farcha.

1. Using a meat hammer, gently flatten each piece of chicken.

2. Evenly prick the surface of the chicken with a fork to ensure the chicken marinates and cooks equally.

3. Mix the chicken with all of the ingredients except the cilantro, egg, and semolina. Marinate in the refrigerator for a minimum of 1 hour.

4. Mix in the cilantro with the semolina and coat each piece of chicken in semolina flour mix.

5. Place a frying pan on medium heat and add the oil.

6. One at a time, dip each piece of flour-coated chicken into the egg white batter and place it in the frying pan.

7. Fry for 6-7 minutes, until the chicken is cooked and the egg coating is golden brown in color.

8. Egg batters tend to soak in more oil than usual so let the cooked pieces rest on a paper towel to absorb any excess oil.

9. Serve immediately with a spicy coriander-mint chutney or dipping sauce of your choice!

Between 8th and 10th century CE, Persian people immigrated from Iran to India to escape persecution during the Arab occupation of Persia. In India, these Persian Indians are referred to as the Parsi community. Parsi cuisine is now famous in Mumbai, having catered to their working-class population. The modern-day Parsi cuisine was especially shaped during the British rule of India when a well-known strip of Parsi restaurants in Mumbai became popular amongst the British.

The main dishes characteristic of a Persian meal are combinations of rice and meat, such as lamb, chicken, or fish. Vegetables like onions and fresh herbs like parsley are also used, along with nuts. Some special dishes are flavored by adding spices like saffron and cinnamon. Parsis love eggs, potatoes and meat. Almost all the vegetable dishes made from okra, tomatoes or potatoes will have eggs on top. Meat dishes will have potatoes in the form of *salli* (matchstick fried potatoes). Dishes like the khichda and dhansak have lentils which are adopted from typically Indian preparation of daal and given a meaty twist to make it their own.

The first time I had Parsi cuisine was at a now popular chain in New Delhi, India. It's a restaurant that was recommended to me by friends as the new kid on the block for popular Indian cuisine. I loved it—the fusion of flavors, the accompanying salads, the subtle usage of Indian spices. I was all in.

Gateway of India—an iconic structure in Mumbai, India. Not far from here are various Iranian and Parsi cafes.

I wanted to have an authentic version of what I had eaten without having to travel down to Mumbai, so on a subsequent trip to India, the flight attendant who was very generous with his alcohol pour, suggested Rustom's to me. He warned that there were no bells and whistles to this restaurant, just original recipes of Parsi dishes.

Rustom's is where I had Chicken Farcha, a popular appetizer regularly served at celebrations like weddings or birthday parties in the Parsi community. The usage of chicken mixed with herbs, spices, and semolina is popular in Gujurati cuisine, the region of India where many Persians settled. The Persians took that base and added their touch of dipping the chicken into egg. The final touch is of British influence—frying it into golden crunchy fried chicken. The dish combines all three cultures onto one plate.

Owner and Chef of Rustom's, Kainaz Contractor, was generous enough to share her family's recipe. I hope you enjoy making Chicken Farcha and sharing a meal with friends the Parsi way!

BURRAH CHICKEN

2 pounds chicken thighs

1 tablespoon roasted cumin

2 teaspoons white vinegar

1 teaspoon lemon juice

1 tablespoon Kashmiri
chili powder

1 tablespoon ginger – minced

1 tablespoon garlic – minced

1 teaspoon salt

2 tablespoons olive oil

1. In a large bowl, mix together all of the ingredients except the chicken.
2. Add the chicken to this marinade and mix well.
3. Cover and let the chicken marinate for at least 4 hours, and up to overnight in the refrigerator.
4. Preheat oven to 400 degrees.
5. Place the chicken in a baking dish and bake for 45-60 minutes, until the chicken is cooked through.

I like the outside of my chicken to be crispy so I leave it in the oven a little longer. Serve Burrah Chicken with lemon wedges, pickled onions, and a salad.

Burrah Chicken at Rajinder da Dhaba, New Delhi, India

When I was younger and traveled to India with my family, I was always told not to have food outside of our hotels because of hygiene. We would end up eating at high-end places due to the fear of getting sick in an attempt to avoid ruining our trip. Once in awhile, we would veer off that path and have juices or pakoras (anything dipped in a batter and fried) from street stalls. Though, I always got sick. It became known in my family that I had a soft stomach, especially in India!

As I grew older, and India became more commercialized with the influx of corporations building offices in major cities, I began to venture outside of the hotel restaurant fare and try foods from landmark establishments. One major establishment is Rajinder da Dhaba in New Delhi. It is a staple pick-up and go hole in the wall that meat eaters flock to for tasty tandoor cooked specialties fit for royalty.

Typically, the wait to get your order at this place is over an hour because of the demand. On any given night, cars pull up, the men will place their orders, have a few drinks by their cars while they wait, and then eat the content of their takeout containers by their cars before heading home. It's an

Long lines of mostly men at Rajinder da Dhaba

experience that usually groups of friends or families come to enjoy.

My mom and I showed up one night while in India, and to our surprise it was not busy at all. I wasn't going to second guess it! We walked into the tiny sit-down portion of the restaurant which had about four tables with chairs and ordered all of the popular items – Burrah Chicken being one of them. The simple spices, grilled smoky flavor, and tartness from the lemon squeezed on top won me over! Since we were the only seated diners at the restaurant on this questionably eerie night, I asked the waiter for the recipe for

this chicken. He was more than happy to share it with me!

We also asked the waiter why it was empty and he told us it was Janmashtmi, one of the most religious Hindu holidays, where even meat eaters give up eating meat for the day. My mom usually practices this holiday, but we had no concept of time while in India. This oversight allowed us the opportunity to try this delicious meal that I'm now happy to share. I hope you enjoy it as much as we did!

Singapore Carrot Cake

1 pound daikon (preferably Chinese daikon)

1 teaspoon white pepper

2 cups finely ground rice flour (not sweet; an Asian brand such as Erawan)

2 cups water

6 large eggs

2 tablespoons chopped garlic

¼ cup ketjap manis (Indonesian sweet soy sauce) or thick soy sauce

1 ½ teaspoons sambal oelek or Sriracha (Southeast Asian chili sauce), plus additional for serving

3 scallions – chopped

½ cup loosely packed fresh cilantro sprigs

2 teaspoons salt

7 tablespoons peanut or vegetable oil

Carrot Cake at Telok Ayer Hawker Market in Singapore– one of the most popular food courts in Singapore

1. To make the daikon cake, oil the bottom and side of a 9-inch round cake pan.

2. Peel the daikon, then shred in a food processor fitted with a medium shredding disk. Reserve any liquid.

3. Heat wok over high heat until a drop of water evaporates instantly. Pour 3 tablespoons of oil down the side of wok, then tilt wok to swirl, coating sides. When oil begins to smoke, add the daikon with any reserved liquid, 1 teaspoon of salt, and ½ teaspoon pepper. Stir-fry for 3 minutes. Cover and cook over moderately low heat, stirring and breaking up the daikon occasionally, until it is very tender, about 15 minutes.

4. Whisk together the rice flour and water in a large bowl until smooth, then stir in the daikon mixture (it will be lumpy) and pour into the cake pan.

5. Set a steamer rack inside cleaned wok and fill wok with water (not above steamer rack); bring to a boil. Reduce heat to moderate and steam cake in pan on rack, covered for 1 hour (replenish water as necessary). Wearing oven mitts, transfer pan to a cooling rack and cool for about 1 ½ hours. Wrap pan tightly with plastic wrap and chill at least 8 hours.

6. To make the stir fry, run a knife along the edge of the cake to loosen, then invert onto a cutting board, tapping on the bottom of pan until cake is released. Blot with paper towels. Cut cake into ½-inch cubes.

7. Beat together eggs, ½ teaspoon salt, and ¼ teaspoon pepper in a bowl. Set aside.

8. Heat dried wok over high heat until a drop of water evaporates instantly. Pour remaining 4 tablespoons of oil down side of wok, then tilt wok to swirl, coating side.

9. When oil begins to smoke, add cake cubes, garlic, remaining ½ teaspoon of salt, and ¼ teaspoon of pepper. Stir-fry, letting cake rest on bottom and sides of wok about 10 seconds between stirs, until golden brown, 8-10 minutes. (Cubes will soften and may stick to wok. Scrape away the brown bits from the bottom of wok and continue stir-frying.)

10. Add eggs and stir-fry until eggs are just set, about 1 minute.

11. Stir in ketjap manis, sambal oelek, and scallions, then transfer to a serving dish and scatter cilantro on top.

Unlike the western version of carrot cake that's sweet and served for dessert, this is a spicy, savory Singaporean version with Chinese daikon, rice flour, and absolutely no carrots, or sugar! Serve with additional sambal oelek if you want it spicier.

Marina Bay Sands in Singapore at night

BBQ Bread Pudding and Avocado Crema

1 large loaf day old bread – cubed

1 tablespoon butter

4 large eggs

1 cup chicken stock (vegetable stock can be used for a vegetarian version)

2 cups heavy cream

2 cups cheddar cheese

1 cup BBQ sauce

1 cup pickled jalapeños

1 cup frozen corn kernels – defrosted

1 cup black beans

1 red onion – finely chopped

2 cups shredded chicken (optional)

2 avocados – peeled and pitted

1 cup cilantro – chopped

2 tablespoons olive oil

Salt to taste

1. Preheat oven to 350 degrees.

2. Heat the oil and butter in a large frying pan on medium-high heat.

3. Add the onions and sauté until translucent.

4. Lower the heat and add the corn, black beans, chicken (if using); mix together well. Stir in the BBQ sauce, mix well, and immediately remove from heat.

5. In a large mixing bowl, whisk together eggs, 1 ½ cups of heavy cream, stock, and 1 ½ cups of cheddar cheese.

6. Add the bread cubes, pickled jalapeños and BBQ mixture; mix well to combine.

7. Set aside at room temperature for 30 minutes to allow the bread to absorb the liquid.

8. Stir well and pour into a large baking dish (9x13 inches).

9. Sprinkle with the remaining cheese and bake for 45-50 minutes, until the top has browned and the bread pudding has set. Push a toothpick through the dish and if it comes out mostly clean, the pudding has set.

10. While the bread pudding is baking, make the avocado crema by combing the avocados, ½ cup of heavy cream, cilantro, and salt in a blender. Transfer to a bowl and refrigerate until ready to use.

Serve this amazing bread pudding hot and topped with the avocado crema. Use as a side to your favorite barbecued meats or alone as a main dish!

TANDOORI CHICKEN WINGS

¼ cup plain yogurt

2 teaspoons garam masala*

1 tablespoon dried
fenugreek leaves*

½ inch knob of
ginger–chopped

3 garlic cloves–chopped

½ teaspoon turmeric

½ teaspoon red chili powder

2 tablespoons
cilantro–chopped

1 beet–boiled and grated

1 pound chicken wings

1 tablespoon olive oil

Salt to taste

*These can be found in South Asian
grocery stores.

1. Preheat oven to 400 degrees.

2. In a medium bowl, combine all of the ingredients except the chicken.

3. Taste the marinade and adjust seasoning as desired. I tend to add more salt after I taste it.

4. Toss in the chicken. Make sure the yogurt marinade evenly coats each wing. Marinate the chicken for at least 2 hours in the refrigerator–overnight will yield the best results.

5. Stack a wire rack on a baking pan. This will give you crispy wings because the fat from the chicken will drain away.

6. Arrange the chicken wings on the wire rack and cook in the oven for about 40-50 minutes.

7. Serve with a cool mixture of yogurt, mint, salt, and cucumber!

TURKISH BREAKFAST EGGS—MENEMEN

8 eggs

1 green bell
pepper – finely sliced

3 scallions – finely sliced

4 medium
tomatoes – finely diced

1 tablespoon butter

4 ounces feta
cheese – crumbled

2 teaspoons pul biber
(or red pepper flakes)

1 tablespoon olive oil

Salt and pepper to taste

1. Heat the butter and the olive oil in a frying pan.

2. Stir in the bell pepper and cook for a couple of minutes, at low to medium heat.

3. Mix together the scallions, tomatoes, and pul biber.

4. Crack the eggs into a bowl and whisk with a fork. Add the feta cheese and combine well.

5. Pour the egg mixture into the frying pan and give it a good stir. Scramble the eggs until they are just done, retaining their juice. Season with salt and fresh ground black pepper to taste.

6. Serve in the frying pan itself with good bread or crepes.

A traditional Turkish breakfast spread with Menemen in the center

Flavor-wise on its own, Menemen is like a Shakshouka or a French Piperade or an Indian Bhurji or some can even argue that it's similar to Huevos Rancheros, but a Menemen is the engine of brunch in Turkey. It is the central point of a traditional breakfast display including an array of sweet, spicy, salty, fried, and rich foods that are meant to be eaten one after the other, with bread of course. One bite salty, one bite sweet, the next bite spicy, the next bite fried, and so on with non-stop Turkish tea poured to fill the gaps. The Turkish breakfast was by far the best breakfast experience I've had and Menemen was at center stage of the lavish spread that brought it all together.

Some people add sausage called sucuk or pastirma which is a Turkish-style pastrami to their version of Menemen. I like adding shredded New York pastrami once in a while to really make an East-meets-west dish. So go ahead and add all of your favorite ingredients!

SHORTCUT COQ AU VIN BLANC

1 cup yellow
onions – finely diced

1½ cups bacon – finely
chopped

3 garlic cloves – minced

2 chicken thighs + 2 chicken
legs (alternatively you can
use 4 chicken breasts)

1 cup baby bella
mushrooms – quartered

1 tablespoon
thyme – chopped

1 tablespoon
parsley – chopped

½ bottle Chenin Blanc
or Riesling (one that you
would drink as well)

1 cup chicken stock

½ cup whole milk

½ cup cream

1 cup fingerling potatoes

2 teaspoons ground
black pepper

4 tablespoons butter

4 tablespoons flour

4 tablespoons vegetable oil

Salt to taste

1. In a heavy-bottomed pan (such as a cast iron skillet), heat the oil on medium-high heat.

2. Season the chicken with salt and pepper and when the oil is hot, brown the chicken pieces on all sides. If the chicken has skin, make sure to brown the skin so it is crispy brown.

3. Remove the chicken from the pan and set aside. Drain the fat used to brown the chicken.

4. In the same pan, add the onion and bacon and fry until the onion has turned translucent and the bacon has rendered all the fat. Add the chopped garlic and sauté for a few minutes.

5. Add the mushrooms and thyme and cook for another 5 minutes.

6. Remove the mushrooms/onion/bacon mixture from the pan.

7. Add the 4 tablespoons of butter and let it melt. Sprinkle the flour and whisk to form a smooth paste. Keep stirring this paste on medium heat without letting it brown, to cook the flour. The paste should turn into a beige color.

8. Return the mushroom/bacon/onion mixture to the pan. Add the Riesling and broth; mix until smooth. Add the chicken and potatoes; bring the mix to a boil.

9. Reduce the heat and simmer on low heat for about 25-30 minutes, or until the chicken and potatoes are cooked through.

10. Mix the milk and cream together in a bowl, then stir the mixture into the pan and let it heat through for another few minutes.

11. Serve immediately with chopped parsley on top and toasted French bread on the side.

Lavender fields in front of Abbaye de Senanque, Provence, France

Literally translating to "Rooster in Wine", Coq au Vin is typically chicken slow-cooked in French Burgundy wine, similar to the peasant dish Boeuf Bourguignon. Versions of Coq Au Vin that use white wine are prevalent in the Eastern part of France, closer to Germany and Switzerland. Braised stews are a favorite not only in France but in many countries because all sorts of meats and root vegetables can be used to make a hearty meal on a low budget. The authentic version of Coq au Vin requires hours of braising so I wanted to share my shortcut version that anyone can make. No one will know that you haven't been cooking in the kitchen for hours!

SOUR CREAM CHIPOTLE ENCHILADAS

3 cups shredded chicken

1 onion – chopped

1 can chipotle peppers packed in adobo – chopped

1 tablespoon tomato paste

1 zucchini – chopped

8 (8-inch) flour tortillas

1 ½ cup cheddar cheese – grated

¼ cup butter

¼ cup flour

15 ounces chicken broth

1 cup sour cream

1 tablespoon olive oil

Jalapeños – deseeded and chopped

1. In a frying pan on medium heat, add the olive oil, cooked chicken, and onion together and stir.

2. Add the tomato paste and chipotle peppers along with the adobo sauce and stir.

3. Remove from heat and mix in the zucchini – the zucchini should stay crunchy.

4. Divide the cooked chicken mixture evenly across 8 tortillas. Add 1 ½ tablespoons of cheese to each tortilla.

5. Roll the enchiladas and place seam-side down in a 9x13-inch baking dish that has been lightly sprayed with no-stick cooking spray.

6. Melt the butter in a medium saucepan. Stir in the flour to make a roux, stirring and cooking until bubbly, then gradually whisk in the chicken broth; bring to boiling, stirring frequently.

7. Remove from heat; stir in sour cream and green chilis.

8. Pour the sauce evenly over the enchiladas.

9. Top with the remaining ¾ cup of cheese. (The baking dish may be double-wrapped and frozen at this point.)

10. Bake at 400 degrees for 20 minutes, until cheese is melted and sauce near the edges of the baking dish is bubbly.

This is my take on a Mexican classic using chipotle peppers, which are some of my favorite peppers to work with. The crunchiness of the zucchini, slight spice from the chipotle peppers, and creaminess of the sour cream sauce bring this dish harmoniously together. These enchiladas are one of my family's favorites!

BELIZEAN CHOCOLATE CHICKEN

6 ounces culantro*

1 ½ pounds desired
cut of chicken

4 ounces 80% dark chocolate

8 ounces coconut cream

1 cup tomatoes – diced

10 ounces tomato sauce

6-8 bird's eye chilis

3 garlic cloves – minced

1 large onion – finely
chopped

1 cup bell pepper – chopped

4 tablespoons olive oil

Salt to taste

*Jarred Goya brand Recaito Culantro
Cooking Base is preferred. Note that
culantro is not the same as cilantro,
although they are cousins. This recipe is
most authentic when culantro is used,
however, if it isn't available you can
use 6 ounces of cilantro mixed with 2
tablespoons of water and 1 teaspoon
of vinegar.

1. In a saucepan on low heat, add 2 tablespoons of olive oil and the garlic. Stir until the garlic turns slightly light brown.

2. Add the onions and sauté until the onions are translucent.

3. Add the bell peppers and sauté until the peppers are soft and the onions start turning slightly brown.

4. Add in 4 ounces of the culantro and chilis. Stir for 2 minutes.

5. Add in the tomatoes and cook until the tomatoes become a mush.

6. Add in the tomato sauce and stir. Add in the chocolate and stir.

7. Add salt to taste, about 2 teaspoons.

8. Now that the sauce is done, in another large frying pan on medium heat, add 2 tablespoons of olive oil and the chicken.

9. Liberally season the chicken with salt. Continue stirring and cooking the chicken until it starts to brown. Cover the pan with a lid and cook for 5-10 minutes until the chicken starts releasing water.

10. Add in the remaining 2 ounces of the culantro and mix well with the chicken. Allow the chicken to cook an additional 2-3 minutes covered.

11. Add the chocolate sauce and stir well with the chicken. Cover and cook for 5-10 minutes on medium heat.

12. Add in the coconut cream, stir well and cover for another 5-10 minutes.

13. You will know the sauce is done when it coats the meat and has a reddish brown color.

Enjoy this delicious and exotic chicken dish with rice or noodles. I like to serve it alongside a refreshing salad made of cucumbers, tomatoes, raw onions and a bit of vinegar.

Cacao pods growing in
the rainforest in Belize

Belize is a tropical Central American and Caribbean country that has deep roots in Mayan Culture. I visited for New Years Eve one year with my best friend and after a few days of soaking in the beach town of Ambergris Caye, we headed to Belize City to learn about the Mayans. We explored the caves, went zip lining, and walked through the ghost town of Belize City. The most exciting part of our week was a trip to the Toledo Region of Belize.

After our one hour chartered flight from Belize City to San Felipe, we arrived at what was the tiniest airport I'd ever been to. Juan, one half of the couple-owner-duo of Ixcacao (pronounced Ish-Ca-Cow) Maya Belizean Chocolate arrived to pick us up and immediately took us to their rainforest farm where the cacao pods grow.

Walking naively through the rainforest, we spotted banana flowers, breadfruit, coconuts, and an abundance of cacao trees. From there, we viewed the local Mayan ruins and learned about their traditions specifically related to sports and hunting. We also saw a few Pará rubber trees that produce latex through rubber tapping. Then Juan told us to beware of snakes, and I made a beeline for the car!

While we were in the rainforest though, I picked a cacao pod and saved it to bring back to the farm. Once we arrived, we were greeted by the roosters

Chocolates, cacao pods, and roasted cacao seeds

roaming the property and Abelina Cho–the second half of the couple-owner-duo. We walked up wooden stairs onto a covered terrace made entirely of wood that had an outdoor kitchen on one side. Abelina had prepared an authentic lunch for us and by then we were starving! I walked through her lunch spread and recognized a few items–vegetarian tamales, beans, mixed salad with vinegar, a chicken that looked like a darker version of chicken curry, and a noodle-like dish.

We helped ourselves to lunch, and I'm sorry, but words cannot describe how incredible this lunch tasted. A bite of this was crunchy, a bite of that salty, a bite spicy, a bit creamy–all food spreads should have this combination! What stood out like a star to me was the chicken. I assumed there was probably cacao in it, but the combination of the cacao

with the other ingredients made this chicken so far apart from anything that I had ever tasted. I needed the recipe. So I started a conversation with Abelina by complimenting her chicken to no end. Little by little, I was able to find out the ingredients in her exquisite chocolate chicken. I made this recipe with my own measurements and method yet I give this recipe to you dedicated to the *Queen of Chocolate*, Abelina!

Kashmiri Paella

1 cup paella Bomba rice*

4 pounds chicken wings

1 cup frozen peas

1 cinnamon stick

2 cardamom cloves

¼ teaspoon saffron threads

1 tablespoon warm milk

2 tablespoons paprika

1 quart chicken broth

¼ teaspoon vinegar

½ cup toasted almonds

½ cup dried cranberries

1 teaspoon salt

2 tablespoons olive oil

Juice of one lemon

Spanish Bomba is the typical rice used to cook paella. If it cannot be found, use Italian Arborio rice, found in most supermarkets. The rice you use should be short and round rather than long-grain.

Tools

Paella pan (although a large flat frying pan can be used)

1. Place the chicken wings in a large bowl and drizzle with 2 tablespoons of olive oil, lemon juice, and vinegar.

2. Add ½ teaspoon of salt and 2 tablespoons of paprika. Mix well so that all of the wings are coated.

3. Put a paella pan on medium-high heat and place the wings in the pan skin-side down. Ensure that all of the oil from the bowl is poured into the pan.

4. Once the first side is brown and crispy, turn over the wings to cook the other side.

5. Once fully cooked and crispy (about 20 minutes), remove all of the wings from the pan except for 8-10 pieces. Cook these longer so they are extra crispy.

6. Keep the wings that cooked longer separate from the rest.

7. Add the cinnamon stick and crushed cardamom to the paella pan and stir for 1 minute.

8. Add the less crispy chicken back to the pan and spread evenly.

9. Add the paella rice and peas to the open spaces in the pan and pour the chicken broth over the entire pan.

10. Sprinkle with some salt and let the rice cook on low to medium heat–do not stir.

11. The rice will be soft when completely cooked, however, cook to your desired doneness.

12. Mix the saffron threads with warm milk and sprinkle over the paella.

13. Place the extra crispy chicken on top of the paella, then sprinkle with toasted almonds and cranberries.

Mercado Central (Central Market), Valencia, Spain

Saffron flowers in Kashmir, India. The most expensive food in the world.

One of the first things I ate when I arrived in Spain was traditional Valencian paella. It was hearty, meaty, and required a nap after consuming–enter the famous Spanish siesta!

It was imperative that I tried making paella and of course, with a twist. I ventured out to Central Market in Valencia, a foodie's paradise, and walked the colorful market lanes to get inspired by the flavors surrounding me–mounds of paprika, stalls full of various types of paella rice, Spanish saffron, all sorts of meats, and spices.

I was there in November and autumn was in full swing. When I think of fall, I think of cranberries, nuts, and warm flavors that create comfort during cool and crisp evenings. The season and seasonings around me inspired me to make a North Indian Kashmiri paella. Kashmir is a state in Northern India where the use of nuts, saffron, cinnamon, and cloves are prevalent in almost all of their cooked dishes.

The saffron grown in Kashmir is the most expensive variety in the world. The combination of flavors in this recipe are a special marriage of: my heritage–Indian, the country where I was living at the time–Spain, and the season–autumn. I made this for about 20 people while in Valencia and it was undoubtedly a hit. I hope you enjoy it too!

CHINESE 5-SPICE BANH MI

For the marinated daikon and carrots

¾ cup sugar

¾ cup distilled white vinegar

3 cups matchstick-size pieces daikon

3 cups matchstick-size pieces peeled carrots

¼ teaspoon salt (rounded)

For the chicken

¼ cup soy sauce

6 garlic cloves – minced

4 shallots – chopped

3 tablespoons fish sauce (nam pla or nuoc nam)

1 tablespoon sugar

3 teaspoons five-spice powder*

6 large skinless boneless chicken thighs

Olive oil

For the sandwiches

6 (6-inch) baguettes – split lengthwise

1 English hothouse cucumber – cut into 6-inch long, ¼-inch thick slices

½ red onion – halved through stem, thinly sliced crosswise, rinsed, and drained well

12 fresh cilantro sprigs

2 jalapeños – thinly sliced crosswise

Additional soy sauce

Mayonnaise

For this recipe, I've used store-bought Chinese five-spice powder, but don't be afraid to get inventive and make your own mixture with the spices listed below!

1. To make the marinated daikon and carrots, whisk the sugar, vinegar, and salt together in a large bowl until dissolved. Add the daikon and carrots and toss to coat. Let it stand at room temperature for at least 2 hours. Keep refrigerated for up to 5 days, if desired.

2. To make the chicken, mix the first 6 ingredients in a large bowl and add the chicken; mix well. Let the chicken marinate for 2 hours in the refrigerator, turning the chicken over after 1 hour.

3. Prepare barbecue or preheat broiler to medium-high heat. Brush grill rack with oil.

4. Remove chicken from marinade and grill or broil chicken until cooked through, about 6 minutes per side. Transfer to a plate and tent with foil to keep warm.

5. To prepare the sandwiches, toast the baguettes and spread liberally with mayonnaise on the bottom halves.

6. Top each with cucumber slices, 1 chicken thigh, drained daikon and carrots, onion slices, and cilantro sprigs.

7. Sprinkle with jalapeño slices, soy sauce, and ground black pepper to taste.

8. Place on the baguette tops, pressing to compact, and serve immediately!

Five-spice powder is a commonly used ingredient in Chinese and Taiwanese cuisine. It encompasses all five flavor profiles—sweet, sour, bitter, pungent, and salty. Based on the name alone, you can probably guess there are five different spices in five-spice powder. These are usually a mixture of: star anise, cloves, Chinese cinnamon, Sichuan pepper and fennel seeds. This isn't a strict list though, and five-spice powder can also include: anise seeds, ginger root, nutmeg, turmeric, cardamom pods, licorice, orange peel, or galangal.

Banh Mi is a typical Vietnamese street sandwich usually made with a pork filling. Many versions of fillings now exist around the world to incorporate the freshness of the pickled daikon and carrot, buttery French bread, and spicy meat. That's essentially what you'll find with this recipe!

EASY MIDDLE EASTERN SHAKSHUKA

16 ounces chopped tomatoes

1 tablespoon cumin powder

1 teaspoon paprika

1 red bell pepper – finely chopped

3 garlic cloves – finely chopped

4 eggs

2 ½ tablespoons olive oil

Salt and pepper to taste

1. Put a frying pan over medium heat and add 2 tablespoons of olive oil.

2. Add the garlic and stir until slightly brown.

3. Add the red bell pepper, cumin, and paprika.

4. Stir the peppers until soft and add the tomatoes. Add salt to taste.

5. Use the spatula to create 4 small holes in the sauce where the tomatoes are covering the bottom of the pan. Add the eggs to the holes.

6. Drizzle remaining olive oil on top and season the eggs with salt and pepper.

7. Cover and cook until your desired doneness for the eggs (look for a slight white film if you want a runny yolk or keep cooking if you prefer the yolk hard).

8. Serve immediately and enjoy with bread, sweet potato wedges and/or bacon!

The first time I tried Shakshuka was at a restaurant in New York City called Balaboosta. I wasn't in love with it – sorry Chef Einat Admony and Stefan Nafziger. I thought the eggs were hard and didn't like the combination of the eggs and tomatoey sauce. Perhaps it was because I had too many mimosas prior to trying it, or it could have been all of that delicious hummus and pita which left me so full and unable to truly taste the Shakshuka in all its glory. Whatever the reason, I walked away unimpressed and unwilling to try it again.

Then I went to Dubai for the first time for a friends wedding. I caught up with an old high school friend who had moved and settled there and while we were having the quintessential high tea at the Bhurj al Arab, I told her that I wanted to eat what she ate – her favorite go-to authentic dish in Dubai. I trusted her judgment because we knew each other in our teens after all and there's something to say about familiarity when traveling to foreign lands. The next day she called me early in the morning and asked if I wanted to grab breakfast at her favorite spot for a post-workout bite. She picked me up and we headed to Souk Al Bahar around 8 a.m.

World famous Dubai fountains

The souk was closed for the most part and no one was shopping or even strolling, but one restaurant called Baker & Spice, situated lakeside right opposite the world famous Dubai fountains, was open. They had pastries, cookies, a coffee bar, a fresh fruit juice station, omelettes to order – the breakfast works! She looked at the menu and said, "I usually get the green juice and Shakshuka, it's my favorite local thing to eat in Dubai, wanna get that?" I paused and said, "Ok, sure." I mean, I did ask her to introduce me to her favorite thing to eat, and if this was it, so be it.

Alcohol isn't sold in most restaurants that are not attached to a hotel in Dubai so this time I wasn't going to be having mimosas to cloud my judgment. The green juice came – it was delicious just as

she mentioned, and on this particular morning I had worked out at the gym, so the cells in my body were loving the nutrient pump. Then came the Shakshuka pan with four poached eggs for us to share and a huge basket of warm and crusty on the outside, soft on the inside bread. I took my bread, broke off a piece, dipped it in the sauce, put some egg on top, took a bite and WOW! In that instance I was converted to a Shakshuka lover! I loved it so much that two years later when I had a seven hour layover in Dubai, I left the airport just to go eat this meal at Baker & Spice!

I've shared my version with you so you too can fall in love with this saucy, protein-packed breakfast. It's delicious with or without mimosas!

Emirati Saloona

2 pounds bone-in chicken – cut into pieces

2 medium onions – finely chopped

2 garlic cloves – crushed

1 ½ teaspoons Bezar spice*

2 fresh juicy tomatoes – chopped

2 potatoes – cut into chunks

1 carrot – finely chopped

1 bunch coriander – chopped

6-8 cups water

1 teaspoon turmeric

¼ teaspoon ground cinnamon

¼ teaspoon ground cardamom

2 whole loomi (or substitute with lemon peel)

1 tablespoon tomato paste

2 tablespoons loomi juice (or use lemon juice)

½ cup corn oil

Salt to taste

If you cannot find Bezar spice in your local market, it's easy to make by roasting 1 tablespoon each of: whole cumin seeds, fennel seeds, coriander seeds, peppercorns, dried red chilis, and 2 cinnamon sticks. Roast stovetop on high heat until the spices become fragrant. Grind together in a spice grinder or blender and add in 1 tablespoon turmeric powder. Store in an airtight container.

1. Put oil in a large pot on medium heat and add chicken, onion, Bezar spice, and salt.
2. Brown the chicken, turning frequently, and add turmeric, cinnamon, cardamom, garlic and both the whole and juiced loomi (or lemon substitutes).
3. Fry for 5-10 minutes on medium heat, then add the remaining ingredients except the coriander.
4. Bring to a boil and cook until the chicken and vegetables are cooked through, about 20-30 minutes.
5. Sprinkle coriander and serve immediately with white rice and salad.

In most homes throughout UAE, Saloona is made daily and is usually served with steamed rice or ra-gagg (thin bread). It is also a popular side dish to accompany fish or other main courses. During Ramadan, it is served only with bread and this combination is called fareed. The vegetables and spices can be adjusted according to personal taste which is what makes every household recipe different. Saloona is traditionally eaten with the right hand or in modern homes, with a spoon.

I visited the Sheikh Mohammed Centre for Cultural Understanding while I was in Dubai and immediately fell in love with learning what their traditional clothes stand for as well as the importance of their cuisine. Upon entering the center, I was transported to the home of a local Emirati. The representatives from the center explained the traditions in households and the pride that the Emirati have in preserving their culture while accepting the explosive modern culture in Dubai. The food was laid out traditionally on top of a long carpet on the floor and shared family-style among all patrons. The taste was on par with Chicken Tortilla Soup (p. 18) and not overpowering in any way – a perfect balance of tart and spice.

While in the cultural center, I was able to take their recipe for the most traditional Saloona. Hope you give it a try!

Emirati Saloona at The Sheikh Mohammed Center
for Cultural Understanding, United Arab Emirates

SOY SAUCE CHICKEN

6-8 full chicken legs – thighs and legs separated

8 tablespoons butter

½ cup soy sauce

¼ cup lemon juice

3 tablespoons black pepper

¼ cup ginger – julienned

1 white onion – sliced

1 bell pepper – sliced

1. In a large frying pan on high heat, add the butter and melt.

2. Then add the chicken and soy sauce. Stir well, reduce the heat to medium, cover, and let the chicken cook for 25 minutes. Stir the chicken in 5 minute intervals.

3. Once the chicken is fully cooked, add the black pepper and lemon juice. Stir well and cook for another 5 minutes to allow the flavors to meld together.

4. Remove the pan from the heat, add ginger and stir well.

5. Add the onions and bell pepper, stir, and serve. The onions and peppers should be slightly crisp.

6. Serve with corn on the cob and potatoes!

My family loves to eat. More than eating, we love cooking and talking about what our next meal is going to be. Yes – it's at home during my childhood where the foodie in me started to bud. My parents own a business and more often than not, my sister, brother, and I would be at home entertaining ourselves while they would be at work making a living. Our options to eat food at home included warming up frozen pizza in a toaster, toasting a bagel, or heating up leftovers in the microwave.

I got bored and I got brave. I actually turned on the stove. What did I make? This very same soy sauce chicken. I was 8 years old – the house became smoky from the sizzle of the chicken and lack of exhaust fan. But there I was cooking a boneless chicken breast, attempting to make my absolute favorite dish that my mom made during my childhood.

With her in the kitchen, I would wait eagerly for it to be done cooking while the table was already set with boiled corn kernels, French fries, a baguette with butter, and ketchup. My ritual was a bite of chicken, a spoon of corn, dip the fry in ketchup, eat some bread, then back to the chicken. It was buttery, salty, peppery, tart, pungent, and crunchy with the vegetables.

At eight years old, when my parents were at work and I didn't like my food options, I cooked my first-ever dish. It was then that I realized that I could just watch someone make something or I could just taste something to try to recreate it. I hope you like my favorite childhood dish! Try it alone or paired with boiled corn and a side of fries like I used to.

MOTI MAHAL BUTTER CHICKEN

For the tandoori chicken

2 ½ tablespoons boiling water

2 whole chickens (2-3 pounds each)

6 tablespoons fresh lemon juice

3 teaspoons salt

1 ½ teaspoons coriander seeds

1 teaspoon cumin seeds

1 inch ginger root – peeled
and coarsely chopped

2 garlic cloves – coarsely chopped

2 cups plain yogurt

1 teaspoon cayenne pepper

5 teaspoons ghee*

1 teaspoon red food coloring (optional)

For the gravy

6-8 large tomatoes

4-5 garlic cloves

½ cup butter

1 cup full cream

½ teaspoon Kashmiri Mirch powder

3-4 fresh green chilis – slit in
half and seeds removed

Pinch of dried fenugreek leaves (optional)

Salt to taste

Ghee is clarified butter that can be found in most grocery stores and South Asian markets. If you cannot find ghee, replace it with butter.

The original Butter Chicken at Moti Mahal in New Delhi, India

1. To make the chicken, pat the chickens completely dry inside and out using a paper towel, then truss the birds securely.

2. Cut 2 slits about ½-inch deep and 1-inch long in the thighs and breasts of each bird with a small sharp knife.

3. Mix the lemon juice with salt and rub all over the chicken, pressing the mixture deeply into the slits. Then place the chicken in the large deep casserole and set aside while preparing the marinade.

4. Toast the coriander and cumin in a small ungreased pan on medium heat. Shake the pan so the spices are continuously moving and are roasted evenly.

5. Pour the seeds into a blender and add ginger, garlic, and 1 ½ tablespoons of yogurt. Blend at high speed until the mixture is reduced to a smooth paste.

6. Pour into a bowl and add the remaining yogurt, cayenne pepper, and food coloring, and mix.

7. Spread the yogurt masala evenly over the chicken, cover with foil, and marinate in the refrigerator for 12-24 hours – the longer the better.

8. Preheat oven to 400 degrees and arrange the chickens on a rack in a shallow roasting pan. Pour any marinade that collected in the roasting pan back onto the chicken, then coat the chickens with 2 ½ teaspoons of ghee each.

9. Roast uncovered on the middle rack for 15 minutes, then reduce the heat to 350 degrees and continue roasting the chicken for 1 hour. The chicken is done when it is pierced and the juice that runs out is pale yellow.

10. Remove the chicken, let it rest for 10-15 minutes, then cut as desired – shredded or in large chunks with the bones.

11. To make the sauce, put the quartered tomatoes and chopped garlic in a blender and make a paste.

12. In a heavy-bottomed frying pan on medium heat, add the butter. Once bubbling, add the tomato garlic paste and cook until the mixture begins to thicken slightly.

13. Add the Kashmiri Mirch powder, salt, and green chilis, and stir to allow the mixture to thicken.

14. Add the pieces of tandoori chicken and stir to coat them with the thickened paste.

15. Lower the heat, add the cream, and continue cooking for another 4-5 minutes ensuring that it does not boil.

16. Serve garnished with a tablespoon of cream and topped with a pinch of Kasoori Methi.

In India, tandoori chicken is roasted in a special clay oven over hot coals called a tandoor. You can get a similar smoky flavor by roasting the chicken in a hooded charcoal grill equipped with a rotating spit.

Follow the recipe and instead of baking in an oven, a few hours before you plan to serve the chicken, light a 2-inch layer of coals in the grill, cover with the hood, and let the charcoal burn until white ash appears on the surface. This may take over an hour. Remove the chicken from the marinade, thread them on the spit, tie the legs and wings onto the spit, and let the chicken cook over the coals for at least an hour. Continue basting the chicken with ghee every 15 minutes. The smoky flavor that this process gives the chicken is what made the early patrons of Moti Mahal coming back for more!

Moti Mahal of Daryaganj in Central Delhi was once, without any argument, the city's best known eating place. It used to attract visitors from all over the world and was the favorite restaurant of former Soviet and Pakistani prime ministers Nikita Khrushchev and Zulfiqar Ali Bhutto, respectively. India's first prime minister, Pundit Jawaharlal Nehru, used Moti Mahal for catering during his service of almost two decades.

What was so special about Moti Mahal? The owners Kundan Lal Jaggi, Kundan Lal Gujral, and Thakur Dass brought the cooking techniques of Peshawar, Pakistan over to Delhi after the partition between India and Pakistan. Moti Mahal was first opened by Mokha Singh in Peshawar and when he was forced to leave after the partition, the restaurant in Peshawar was closed. It was at Moti Mahal's Peshawar location where Kundan Lal Jaggi and Kundan Lal Gujral both worked as waiters. Thakur Dass was a neighbor whose family had a rice and lentils business across the road.

After the restaurant closed, Mr. Jaggi left his wife to stay with his in-laws in Sonam near Patiala and came to Delhi along with two former associates he met in Peshawar. While he was roaming around in the Roshanara Road area he saw both his former co-worker Kundan Lal Gujral and his former neighbor Thakur Dass by sheer coincidence. They had been buying a bottle of whisky at a shop and decided to celebrate the reunion. Gujral suggested that it was time for them to start a business together. The trio had to fend for themselves and it was a matter of survival. They were advised that the best business to create a new beginning was a food business so they started looking for a place.

After scouting a few locations, they came to Daryaganj where a Sikh man offered to sell them a shop he had occupied on the main road. The trio raised Rs 6,000, a princely sum in 1947, and started a tea shop. Mr. Jaggi toasted the bread and Gujral made the tea.

While exploring Roshanara Road, "We discovered that there were food shops doing good business and were fortunate that a meat shop opened nearby and the vegetable mandi was already in the area."

Mr. Jaggi said that he recruited some more people he knew from Peshawar, and with Mokha Singh's blessing to use the name Moti Mahal, the food institution in Delhi was born. The three were brothers in the operation and divided the work. Jaggi was the hands-on man, Gujral looked after public relations and Thakur Dass did all the shopping for provisions and raw material.

The initial dishes served at Moti Mahal were mostly tandoori cooked meats like Tandoori Murga and Tandoori Fish. The specialty dish was a huge "family naan", served straight from the clay oven and large enough to feed a whole family. The initial phenomena of Moti Mahal was that it brought a new eating out culture to Delhi, something with which the people were totally unfamiliar. It was the place to be seen and the fame of Moti Mahal spread rapidly.

Moti Mahal invented a number of dishes including Chicken Pakoda and Dal Makhani but what Moti Mahal is most famous for is their invention of Butter Chicken. It was invented by accident one evening when a customer came late in the evening and asked for their Tandoori Murga, or tandoori chicken. This chicken itself was unique since it was cooked in a clay oven, where hot smoke flavored with chicken drippings absorbed into the chicken and created an unparalleled flavor. Mr. Jaggi said, "There used to be at least 200 chickens (no broilers those days) which would go into the tandoor and it was a combination of spices and smoke that did the trick."

The customer asked for some gravy with the chicken and since the restaurant was about to close there was very little food left except for the creamy and buttery tomato-based gravy used to make Dal Makhani. Mr. Jaggi poured the gravy over the chicken and a few minutes later the customer was licking the plate clean. This new dish was placed on the menu and the love for it became a phenomena not only in New Delhi but, internationally. Today it is the most ordered dish in Indian restaurants around the world.

The exterior of Moti Mahal in New Delhi, India

The recipe differs in each restaurant and Moti Mahal's focus on quality has been compromised for shortcut methods.

Mr. Jaggi said that the reason behind the success of Moti Mahal can be attributed to the unflinching desire to succeed amongst the three partners who had bonded with each other so well after seeing horrific times during and in the aftermath of partition.

In Delhi, if we find the magic missing today, it is because the Peshawari cooks have been replaced by those who lack the same kind of touch and dedication as Mr. Jaggi and his partners who sold off their business in Daryaganj. It is also the effect of changing times and palates. However, Moti Mahal Daryaganj of the 1950s, 1960s and 1970s was, without any exaggeration, Delhi's unsurpassable eating place.

I had the pleasure of speaking with Mr. Jaggi on recounting his story and he was kind enough to share the original recipe of Moti Mahal's Butter Chicken with me. Make sure you have enough naan for this feast!

SHAN NOODLES

2 pounds ground chicken

2 tablespoons paprika

½ teaspoon cayenne

½ teaspoon turmeric

1 teaspoon Chinese five-spice powder

2 white onions – finely chopped

10 garlic cloves – finely minced

2 tablespoons soy sauce

2 large tomatoes – finely diced

1 ½ cups large rice noodles

½ cup peanuts – crushed

½ cup green onions – thinly sliced

½ cup pickled mustard greens (optional)*

1 teaspoon salt

¼ cup peanut oil

All of the ingredients, including the pickled mustard greens, should be available at your local Asian grocery store. However, if the mustard greens are not available, omit them.

1. In a wok or large frying pan, heat the oil over medium-high heat. Add the onions and sauté until the onions start to turn slightly brown. Stir in the garlic, lower the heat to medium, and stir for another 3-4 minutes.

2. Add in the tomatoes. Stir until the tomatoes have released their water and have mixed completely into the onion-garlic mixture.

3. Add the ground chicken, paprika, cayenne, turmeric, five-spice powder, and salt. Stir to mix really well. Brown the chicken until it is completely cooked.

4. Remove from the heat and add in soy sauce. Taste and adjust seasoning if needed.

5. Bring water to a boil in a large saucepan and drop in the rice noodles. Cook for about 10 minutes while stirring often to prevent sticking. Drain the noodles in a colander and rinse with cold water.

6. Transfer the noodles to a serving bowl, top with the chicken and sauce, and sprinkle with peanuts, green onions, and pickled mustard greens if using.

Shan Noodles are the most popular noodle dish from Shan, the eastern state of Myanmar, and there are two types – dry or wet. The wet type is more of a noodle soup, whereas the dry type has a pasta Bolognese consistency. I prefer the dry type – easy to make and packed with flavor, it's a perfect weeknight dinner!

The calmness of Myanmar

CHAWLA'S CREAM CHICKEN

1 pound boneless chicken – cubed

1 medium onion – chopped

2 tablespoons jeera

1 tablespoon black pepper

½ cup kasoori methi

1 tablespoon dried coriander

2-3 cinnamon sticks

2 cups fresh cream

2 green chilis – sliced lengthwise

1 cup milk

2 teaspoons cornflour

1 tablespoon vegetable oil (or ghee)

Salt to taste

1. Dry roast the jeera, coriander, kasoori methi, cinnamon, and black pepper. Let it cool, then grind to make masala powder. Set aside.

2. Add oil or ghee to a frying pan, along with the onions and chilis.

3. When the onions turn slightly brown, add the cream, milk, 3 tablespoons of the roasted masala and chicken.

4. Cook on medium heat until the chicken comes to a boil.

5. Add salt and 1 tablespoon of masala; cook on low heat.

6. When the chicken is cooked through, about 15 minutes, add the cornflour mixed with a few drops of cold water and stir well until the gravy is thick.

7. Cook for another 2-3 minutes and serve hot with rice or naan.

A visit to the Indian state of Punjab is incomplete without trying this creamy chicken. I hope you also enjoy making it at home!

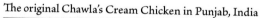

The original Chawla's Cream Chicken in Punjab, India

FRENCH EGGS EN COCOTTE

1 cup cremini
mushrooms – sliced

1 tablespoon butter

1 teaspoon fresh thyme
leaves – chopped

2 eggs

4 teaspoons heavy cream
(or double cream)

2 tablespoons Parmesan
cheese – freshly grated

6 cups boiling water

Baguette – toasted to serve

Salt and pepper to taste

Drizzle of truffle
oil (optional)

1. Preheat oven to 350 degrees. Rinse the mushrooms well.

2. Melt the butter in a frying pan on high heat. As soon as it stops foaming, add the mushrooms, thyme, and a little salt and pepper.

3. Fry the mushrooms over high heat for 5 minutes, until golden and their juices have thickened and reduced.

4. Divide the mushrooms between two 8-ounce ramekin dishes.

5. Add 2 teaspoons of Parmesan on top of the mushrooms and break an egg into each one.

6. Top with equal portions of the cream, Parmesan, and a little salt and pepper.

7. Place the ramekins in a deep ovenproof tray and add enough boiling water to come halfway up the sides of the dishes.

8. Bake for 10-15 minutes, until the top is slightly golden and the eggs are cooked to your liking.

9. To achieve the perfect balance of set white and soft yolk, check the progress after 10 minutes, cooking a little longer as necessary.

10. Cool for 5 minutes. Serve with baguette and a drizzle of truffle oil, if desired.

The name of this dish references the vessel in which it is cooked, the cocotte. Referred to as Oeufs en Cocotte in France, the cocotte is a small heatproof dish in which individual food can be prepared and served – an individually-sized dutch oven. In this recipe I've suggested using the larger ramekins as they are more versatile and affordable to keep in your kitchen.

This is a breakfast that I make when I want to feel a bit more elegant in the morning!

Khao Soi

1 whole dried bird's eye chili (or 1 whole chile de arbol)

2 whole small shallots—peeled and split into quarters

4 whole garlic cloves

1 lemongrass stalk—bottom 4 inches only, roughly chopped

1 teaspoon lime zest (or 2 whole lime leaves, or 2 teaspoons lime juice)

1 tablespoon turmeric powder

1 teaspoon ginger powder

1 cup cilantro—chopped

1 teaspoon whole coriander seeds

1 green cardamom—inner seeds only

1 ½ tablespoons Thai shrimp paste

1 pound fresh Chinese-style egg noodles—divided

2 (15-ounce) cans coconut milk

1 cup low-sodium chicken stock

2 tablespoons palm sugar or brown sugar

4 full chicken legs—split into drumsticks and thighs

½ teaspoon fish sauce

1 cup vegetable or canola oil

Kosher salt

Optional garnishes

Sliced shallots

Lime wedges

Pickled Chinese mustard root

Note: Palm sugar, Thai shrimp paste and pickled mustard greens can be found in most Asian food markets.

1. Place chili, shallots, garlic, lemongrass, lime zest, turmeric, ginger, cilantro, coriander seeds, and cardamom in the bottom of a wok or cast iron skillet. Heat over high heat, turning occasionally until smoky, about 10 minutes. Allow contents to cool slightly and transfer to a large mortar and pestle or a spice grinder.

2. Add 1 teaspoon salt and the shrimp paste to the aromatics and pound until a very fine paste is formed, about 10 minutes. Set the curry paste mixture aside.

3. Separate a quarter of the noodles (enough noodles to make a crispy fried noodle topping for 4 bowls) and set the remaining noodles aside.

4. Heat the vegetable oil in a large wok over high heat until shimmering. Working in batches, add the noodles to oil and fry, stirring and flipping until golden brown and crisp. Transfer to a paper towel-lined plate, season with salt, and set aside.

5. Discard all but 1 tablespoon of oil from the wok. Add the curry paste mixture and cook, stirring the paste into the oil for 1-2 minutes. Add 1 can of coconut milk to the wok and stir for another 2 minutes, until the oil separates from the paste and coconut mixture.

6. Slowly whisk in the second can of coconut milk, followed by the chicken stock and palm sugar. Add the chicken legs and lower the heat to a simmer. Cook the chicken until completely tender, about 30 minutes. Add ½ teaspoon of fish sauce.

7. Bring a pot of salted water to a boil. Add remaining uncooked noodles and cook until al dente, about 1 minute. Drain the noodles and divide between four warm bowls. Top the noodles with two pieces of chicken.

8. Divide the broth evenly between bowls. Top with fried noodles and serve immediately with sliced shallots, lime wedges, and pickled mustard greens on the side.

Khao Soi hails from Chiang Mai, a culinary capital in Northern Thailand. This recipe has an immense amount of flavor while balancing all aspects of sweet, spicy, crunchy, and tart. I tried this dish on a whim as my first dinner in Chiang Mai years ago. It was a rainy night and this was the perfectly-comforting meal that I was looking for – for that, it stuck in my memory. While it can take some time to make, I think it's a great Sunday supper!

PORK

TANDOORI BACON BLT

1 pound bacon

1 beefsteak tomato – sliced

¼ head iceberg lettuce

½ cup mayonnaise

8 slices thick white bread

2 tablespoons tandoori
Spice Mix

For the tandoori spice mix

1 teaspoon ground ginger

1 teaspoon ground cumin

1 teaspoon ground coriander

1 teaspoon paprika

1 teaspoon turmeric

1 teaspoon cayenne pepper

1 teaspoon garlic powder

1 teaspoon ground nutmeg

1 teaspoon salt

1. Mix together all of the spices for the tandoori spice mix, then store in an airtight jar.

2. Preheat oven to 375 degrees. Place the bacon strips in a foil-lined baking pan. Sprinkle 2 tablespoons of the spice mix on both sides of the bacon.

3. Bake in the oven for 15 minutes to make crispy bacon.

4. To assemble the sandwiches, toast the 8 slices of bread.

5. Spread 1 tablespoon of mayo on each slice of toasted bread (more or less, to taste).

6. Add 1 slice of lettuce to 4 pieces of mayo-covered toast.

7. Add 2 slices of tomato on top of the lettuce.

8. Arrange 3 slices of bacon evenly on top of the tomatoes. (Break bacon slices in half to fit, if needed.)

9. Add another slice of lettuce on top of the bacon.

10. Place remaining 4 pieces of mayo-covered toast on top to finish the sandwiches.

This is my Indian twist on a classic – enjoy!

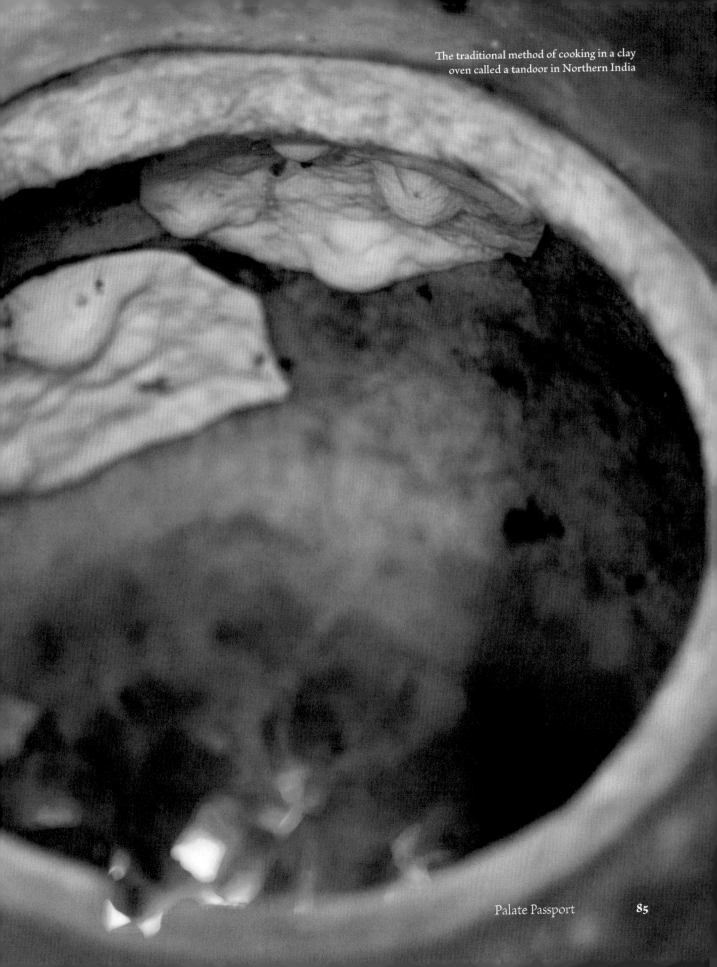

CUBAN EGG ROLLS

1 tablespoon ground cumin

1 tablespoon dried oregano

1 teaspoon ground
black pepper

½ teaspoon crushed
red pepper

5 garlic cloves – minced

3 tablespoons lime juice

3 tablespoons orange juice

3 pounds pork shoulder

8 (7-inch) egg roll wrappers

2 tablespoons water
mixed with a little flour

½ pound store-bought
honey ham – sliced

½ pound Swiss
cheese – sliced

1 cup dill pickles – chopped

1 red onion – thinly sliced

2 tablespoons mustard,
for dipping

2 tablespoons mayonnaise,
for dipping

1 tablespoon salt

2 tablespoons olive oil

1. In a bowl combine the olive oil, salt, cumin, oregano, black pepper, red pepper, garlic, lime juice, and orange juice; mix well.

2. Make little slits in the pork to allow the marinade to seep in. Rub the pork liberally with the oil mixture.

3. Put the pork shoulder in a slow cooker and pour the remaining oil mixture in.

4. Slow cook for 6 hours on low.

5. Remove the meat from the slow cooker and let it cool. Shred the pork using 2 forks.

6. In a separate bowl, combine the ham, cheese, pickles, and onions; mix well.

7. Lay down one egg roll wrapper with a corner pointed toward you. Place 1 tablespoon each of both the pork and ham mixtures.

8. Close the egg roll by folding the corner facing you up and over the mixture. Fold left and right corners toward the center and continue to roll. Brush a bit of the flour paste on the final corner to help seal the egg roll.

9. Place the egg rolls into heated oil and fry, turning occasionally, until golden brown. Remove from the oil and drain on paper towels or a rack.

10. Mix the mustard with the mayonnaise and serve with the eggrolls.

Cuba—a place with so much political controversy, yet much to be desired in terms of old world charm and preservation of the country. Vintage cars, street-side dancing, a lack of commercial hotels, and an environment with little development gives a certain draw for tourists coming from all over the world.

While I haven't visited Cuba, I have been to southern Florida—Miami, Naples, the Keys, Tampa, etc. What I learned was that the popular Cuban sandwich is not from Cuba at all! It originated in Tampa to satisfy factory workers. Based on discussions with various restaurant owners who serve Cuban sandwiches in Miami, there is some debate to this. One Cuban woman I spoke to said, "Some locals claim it was a cheap and satisfying lunch in Cuba for cigar factory workers who then brought the sandwich to the States as a taste of home. However, it is known in Florida that the sandwich gained wild popularity starting in the 1960s when a large influx of Cuban immigrants came to Miami to escape Fidel Castro's reign."

For me a trip to Miami is not complete without having a Cuban sandwich. I thought that nothing could be better than to turn it into a crunchy fried appetizer. When I make these, I serve them alongside black bean soup. And if you're thirsty, a little mojito never hurt anyone!

BUBBLE AND SQUEAK

1 tablespoon butter

4 slices bacon – roughly chopped

1 white onion – finely sliced

1 garlic clove - minced

2 cups Brussels sprouts (or leftover boiled cabbage) – shredded

2 cups leftover mashed potatoes (or cold crushed boiled potatoes)

1. Melt the butter in a non-stick pan on medium heat, then add the bacon. As the bacon begins to brown, add the onion and garlic.

2. Next, add the shredded Brussels sprouts or cabbage and let it brown slightly for about 5 minutes.

3. Add the potato and mix everything together in the pan.

4. Once mixed well, push down so that the mixture covers the base of the pan. Allow the mixture to brown on the base of the pan before turning it over and doing the same on the other side.

5. Cut into wedges and serve!

Bubble and Squeak is a traditional English dish made with leftovers from Sunday roast. The name comes from the sounds that the cabbage and potatoes make when cooking.

I love this dish because I'm a big fan of using leftovers for breakfast. I like to eat this with poached eggs and sautéed mushrooms, but you can really eat this as a side with anything – leftover steak, Sunday's roast, etc.

English countryside, UK

MEXICO CITY PAMBAZOS

6 large bolillos or French baguettes with a hard crust

1 pound ground chorizo

4 large red potatoes

2 cups lettuce – shredded

½ cup Mexican crema (or sour cream)

½ cup crumbled Cotija or Monterey Jack cheese

4 large dried guajillo peppers

½ cup tomatoes – chopped

1 garlic clove

1 cup chicken stock

1 tablespoon olive oil

Hot sauce of your choice

Salt to taste

1. Fill a small saucepan with water and bring to a boil over high heat. Remove from heat and add the guajillo peppers to the water.

2. Let them soak for 20-30 minutes until completely reconstituted. Remove from the water, devein, and deseed the peppers.

3. Place the guajillo peppers, tomatoes, garlic, and chicken stock into a blender; puree until a thin sauce has formed. Pour the sauce into a bowl big enough to dip the entire baguette.

4. Boil the potatoes with the skin on until they are fully cooked and a knife cuts all the way through. Remove the potatoes from the water and mash with a fork.

5. In a frying pan, add the chorizo and fry until it turns slightly crispy. Add in the potatoes, stir and cook for another 10 minutes. Add salt to taste, remove from heat and set aside.

6. Cut each piece of bread and dip each half in the hot pepper paste – make sure both sides are covered.

7. Put 1 tablespoon of oil in a frying pan on medium heat. Once heated, add each piece of bread and fry each side for about 2 minutes, until crispy. Remove each piece of bread and drain on a paper towel.

8. Assemble the pambazo by lining up the bottom portions of each sandwich, stuffing them with a hefty spoon of the chorizo-potato mixture, and topping with lettuce, sour cream, cheese, and hot sauce of your choice.

Pambazo is the name of the bread used to make the traditional version of these sandwiches. Pambazos are found all over the streets of Mexico City and even in bakeries. The signature red coloring of the sandwich is what grabs the attention of hungry purveyors passing by. A beer goes perfectly with these Mexican street bites. Just a word of warning – you will need many napkins because your hands will be drenched in sauce as you enjoy your Pambazo – pure bliss!

Pimenta or Allspice is one of the most important ingredients in Caribbean cuisine and essential to Jerk cooking.

JERK PORK CHOPS

½ cup allspice/pimenta

½ cup brown sugar

8 garlic cloves

3 Scotch bonnet peppers

2 tablespoons thyme leaves

2 bunches scallions – chopped

1 teaspoon cinnamon

½ teaspoon nutmeg

2 tablespoons soy sauce

2 tablespoons lime juice

6 large lean pork chops

2 tablespoons olive oil

1. Place all of the ingredients, except for the pork chops, in a food processor. Blend the ingredients until a liquid paste has formed.
2. Place the pork chops in a large ziplock bag and pour in the marinade. Shake around the pork chops to make sure they are all coated in the marinade.
3. Marinate the meat for at least 12 hours.
4. Preheat the grill on medium heat and oil the grill grate.
5. Arrange the chops on the grate and discard the marinade.
6. Cover and cook the chops for 6-8 minutes on each side.
7. Remove from the grill and let the meat rest for at least 10 minutes.

Since most people automatically associate jerk cuisine with Jamaica, you may be surprised to know that jerk cuisine actually came from the method of cooking used by the Arawak Indians in South America, hundreds of years ago. Usually when someone refers to Jamaican jerking they are referring to a wet marinade that includes pimenta and Scotch bonnet peppers or habanero.

I tried jerk-everything while in Jamaica – jerk pork, jerk lobster, jerk chicken, to list a few, and my favorite way to use jerk cooking is with these pork chops! Serve them with your favorite relish and salad.

Goan Chorizo Pulao

1 pound chorizo – crumbled

1 cup basmati rice

1 cup onions – chopped

1 cup tomatoes – chopped

10 garlic cloves – minced

3 green chilis – slit

1 teaspoon turmeric powder

¼ cup cilantro – chopped

¼ teaspoon white vinegar

2 cloves

4 black peppercorns

1 cinnamon stick

2 bay leaves

½ teaspoon jeera (optional)

1 tablespoon olive oil

Pinch of sugar

Water as required

Salt to taste

1. Soak the rice for 15 minutes. Drain and set aside.

2. In a large saucepan on medium heat, add olive oil, cloves, black peppercorns, cinnamon stick, bay leaves, and jeera.

3. Once it splutters, add the minced garlic, slit green chilis, turmeric, and onions. Sauté until it becomes golden brown.

4. Add in the vinegar; continue to stir and cook for another 5 minutes.

5. Add in the crumbled chorizo; fry on low heat until the meat starts releasing its fat.

6. Add the rice and sauté gently until the rice mixes well with the chorizo and released fat.

7. Add just a pinch of sugar and stir.

8. Add enough water to cover about an inch above the rice.

9. Cook on low heat until the rice has cooked completely.

10. Once the rice has cooked, stir in the fresh cilantro and any additional salt, if needed.

Serve the pulao as a side to your favorite fish dish or even as a meal by itself.

Goan chorizo hung at a local market in Goa, India

I went to Goa, India for a friends wedding. It was my first time visiting and I had heard so much about the beach town from watching Bollywood movies and friends and family that visited. I heard about the draw of hippies because of drugs being readily available, the party scene, the beautiful beaches, and delicious seafood.

What no one talks about is the fact that the Portuguese invaded and owned that region of India for over 50 years. What resulted was pretty churches, a larger Indian Christian community, and fusion cuisine. I had never thought about how largely the history of Goa had impacted it's present day cuisine; in fact, I never thought through that for any city that I visited. When we think of fusion cuisine, we think of flavors that people have combined through their own creativity and imagination.

In Goa, a serious fusion of flavors and ingredients has already existed for a long time due to its tumultuous history. Portuguese flavors are so strong and Indian flavors are so bold with different spices that the combination of the two is explosive.

Everywhere I walked in town I would see strings of chorizo piled on street stalls and so I had to try it. The moment when I saw Chorizo Pulao on a menu, ordered it and ate it, is when it clicked for me that history plays a piv-

A beach in Goa, India at night

otal role in the cuisine of a place. It changed how I viewed cuisine – everywhere that I went I started looking for the backstory.

Chorizo was brought to India by the Portuguese as a cured meat that could be kept on their ships on the way over and consumed while in India as well. When the locals in Goa tried the sausage, they fell in love and just had to make their own version. They learned how to make chorizo from the Portuguese, and once that process was nailed down, they added their own spices.

Goan chorizo is spicier than Portuguese chorizo, and has flavors associated with Indian cuisine such as Kashmiri chilis, turmeric, cumin, and cloves. When cooked with a bit of water and sliced onions, the chorizo releases a bright red color into the dish making a signature curry. The chorizo and onion mixture is eaten with a Portuguese style of bread called Pao – it's heavenly.

Pulao is typically referred to as a rice mixture in India and is derived from the Sanskrit word *Pulāka* (a ball of rice). I have included my version of Chorizo Pulao here where any type of chorizo works great, however, if you want to try the authentic flavors that I tasted in Goa – get out there and find a grocery that sells Goan Chorizo!

GOAN PULLED PORK

15 Kashmiri chilis

1 onion – chopped

6 garlic cloves

1 (1-inch) knob of ginger

2 teaspoons Jeera

1 ½ teaspoons turmeric

1 cinnamon stick

6 peppercorns

6 cloves

½ cup apple cider vinegar

½ cup chicken stock

4 pounds boneless
pork shoulder

1 tablespoon olive oil

Salt to taste

Tools

Slow cooker or cast
iron Dutch oven

Pork Vindaloo cooked at a local's home in Goa

1. Pour 2 tablespoons of olive oil into a slow cooker. Add the onions, garlic, and ginger and stir.

2. Add the pork shoulder, then pour in the apple cider vinegar and chicken stock.

3. Add all remaining ingredients, stir, cover, and cook for 5-6 hours. Cook on high in a slow cooker or on medium heat if cooking over a stovetop. The pork will be done once the meat shreds easily with a fork.

4. Once the meat is done cooking, remove it from the pot and shred all of the meat with a fork.

5. Return the meat to the pot and stir the meat into the juices. Add salt to taste.

With any country, you can find traces of its history in its cuisine. Pork Vindaloo, famed for its fiery heat, is actually a dish that was created during the Portuguese occupation of the southern Indian state of Goa. Carne de vinha d'alhos, a Portuguese dish made with pork, was the basis of the now-famous vindaloo served in Indian restaurants. Even though Pork Vindaloo is synonymous with Goan food, its name is derived from Portugal – vin is for the vinegar and alho means garlic in Portuguese.

I wanted to make this Goan classic in a way that is familiar to western culture – slow cooking and shredding it! I typically serve this pulled pork on tortillas like a taco or on buns with my favorite fixins.

ANDOUILLE RED BEAN PULAO

1 onion – chopped

1 cup sausage (andouille or chorizo) – chopped

2 garlic cloves – minced

½ cup cilantro – chopped

1 tablespoon tomato paste

1 teaspoon smoked paprika

2 cups canned kidney beans

2 cups cooked quinoa

1½ cups chicken stock

1 tablespoon olive oil

1. In a frying pan on medium heat, add 1 tablespoon of olive oil, onions and garlic. Stir until the onions are translucent.

2. Add the sausage and stir until the sausage has browned.

3. Add the tomato paste and paprika, stir, then add the kidney beans and chicken stock.

4. Stir and cook until the sauce thickens and the beans start releasing starch – the mixture should be slightly soupy.

5. Add in the quinoa and chopped cilantro; stir and serve.

Andouille sausage is a staple ingredient in Cajun cuisine and also Creole cuisine, which represents a diverse mix of French, Spanish, German, West African, and Native American cultures. History books will tell you that both Germany and France had an impact on present day Louisiana, two countries who take great pride in their sausage products. Andouille was brought to Louisiana by French Canadian immigrants in an effort to bring culinary influence to the land they owned in the Americas.

French andouille is typically flavored with onions and some spice whereas the Louisiana version of andouille is highly-spiced and generally goes through two rounds of smoking. Sliced andouille was added as one of the key ingredients in Louisiana classics such as gumbo and jambalaya.

Having eaten both versions, I prefer the Louisiana kind due to the intense flavors found in a single bite. When I visited New Orleans, red beans and rice were served with almost every dish that I ordered. In some restaurants, the red beans arrived with a slice of andouille sausage on top, but I never felt that little sliver was enough. There is an immense smokiness that is added to this dish just by including a little more andouille sausage than the typical plate offers.

The quinoa is my attempt to make it a little healthier. Serve with grilled shrimp or top with a fried egg.

NEW ORLEANS MUFFALETTA

⅔ cup green olives – pitted and coarsely chopped

⅔ cup Kalamata olives – pitted and coarsely chopped

½ cup pimiento peppers – chopped

½ cup hot cherry peppers – coarsely chopped

3 garlic cloves – minced

1 anchovy fillet – mashed

2 tablespoons capers – drained and rinsed

½ cup fresh parsley leaves – finely chopped

1 teaspoon fresh oregano leaves – finely chopped

½ teaspoon fresh ground pepper

½ cup extra virgin olive oil

1 large round bread loaf (at least 10-12 inches in diameter)

¼ pound salami – thinly sliced

¼ pound capicola – thinly sliced

¼ pound mortadella – thinly sliced

¼ pound provolone – thinly sliced

1. Place the first 11 ingredients in a bowl and mix well. Reserve this olive salad in the refrigerator until ready to use.

2. To assemble the sandwich, cut the bread lengthwise and if especially thick, tear out some of the doughy inside. Lay the bread slices face-up on the cutting board.

3. Spoon the olive mixture onto both halves of the bread.

4. Layer the meat and cheese onto the bottom half, then close with the top half.

5. Cut the sandwich into quarters and serve immediately, or for better flavor, wrap in plastic and allow the bread to soak up juices for 1 hour before serving.

The Mardis Gras Parade in New Orleans, Louisiana

A traditional-style Muffaletta sandwich consists of a muffaletta-style loaf (a round loaf somewhat similar to focaccia, except lighter on the inside), mortadella, salami, mozzarella, ham, provolone, and a signature olive spread. It hails from New Orleans yet has Italian origins due to the Italian immigrants that settled in the bayou.

What makes the sandwich particularly unique from place to place is its signature olive spread, along with the quality of meats used. The signature olive spread consists of olives chopped with a slew of other pickled vegetables such as carrots and cauliflower; basically what one would find in a bottle of Italian Giardiniera, with olives added.

Unlike other sandwiches with wet ingredients that encourage you to serve the sandwich right away to avoid sogginess, this sandwich pretty much requires a little resting time for all of the flavors to truly marry.

DETROIT STYLE PIZZA

A specific Detroit-style pizza pan with angled edges will make authentic Detroit-style pizza, but a regular 8x10-inch baking pan will also work for this recipe.

6 ounces Brick cheese – grated*

6 ounces Mozzarella cheese – grated

12 ounces pepperoni – thinly sliced

4 ounces pickled banana peppers

For the dough

11 ounces bread flour

1 teaspoon instant yeast

8 ounces water

1 tablespoon salt

Extra virgin olive oil as needed

For the sauce

2 teaspoons dried oregano

1 teaspoon red pepper flakes

1 (28-ounce) can high quality crushed tomatoes

2 garlic cloves – minced

2 teaspoons garlic powder

1 teaspoon onion powder

1 teaspoon salt

2 tablespoons extra virgin olive oil

If you cannot find Brick cheese, which is traditionally used to make the pizza, use Monterey Jack cheese.

1. To make the dough, combine the flour, yeast, and salt in a large bowl. Whisk to combine, then add water and stir with a wooden spoon until a round ball of dough has formed. Set aside for 10 minutes.

2. Turn dough onto a countertop and knead until a smooth, silky ball has formed, about 10 minutes.

3. Transfer dough to a bowl, form a tight ball, tightly cover with plastic wrap, and set aside in a warm place until the dough has roughly doubled in volume, about 2 hours.

4. Pour 2 tablespoons of olive oil onto the bottom of a Detroit-style pizza pan or 8x10-inch baking pan. Transfer the dough to the pan. Turn to coat in oil and then press down to try to get the dough to reach the edges of the pan. It will not reach all the way to the edges of the pan this time, but spread as far as you can without tearing the dough. Tightly cover in plastic and set aside for 30 minutes.

5. Press down on the dough again to try and get it to reach the edges. If it doesn't reach the edges, cover and let it rest longer and repeat. It is important that the dough doesn't tear.

6. When the dough is stretched all the way to the corners, cover and set aside to rest while making the sauce. Preheat oven to 550 degrees.

7. To make the sauce, heat 2 tablespoons of olive oil in a medium saucepan over medium heat, until shimmering.

8. Add minced garlic, oregano, and pepper flakes and stir until fragrant, about 30 seconds.

9. Add tomatoes, garlic powder, and onion powder. Bring to a simmer and cook until reduced to about 3 cups, about 30 minutes. Season to taste with salt.

10. To assemble, press down on dough with your fingertips to remove any large air bubbles. Lay half of the pepperoni evenly over the face of the dough.

11. Top with cheese, spreading it evenly and all the way to the edges of the pan. Add remaining pepperoni and banana peppers.

12. Spoon the sauce over surface in 3 even rows. Not all of the sauce will be used on one pie; reserve the rest to make another pizza.

13. Transfer to oven and bake until edges are black and bubbly and exposed cheese on top is starting to brown, 12-15 minutes.

14. Remove the pan and transfer to a kitchen towel on a countertop.

15. Run a thin metal spatula all the way around the edges of the pan to loosen the pizza. Carefully lift it out and slide it onto a cutting board. Cut pizza and serve.

We're here to pay tribute to the most superior of deep dish pizzas of recent times: Detroit's deep dish pizza.

The automotive roots of Detroit played a huge role in the evolution of this new square pizza craze! The story goes that in 1946 Gus Guerra was looking to add new menu items to his struggling neighborhood bar, Buddy's Rendezvous at 6 Mile and Conant, and acquired a few unused blue steel industrial utility trays from a friend who worked at an automotive factory. He was thinking pizza.

He thought the trays would make a good Sicilian-style pizza because of their rectangular shape. He happened to be right—all of the characteristics that make Detroit deep dish pizza distinctly different from Sicilian pizza is the result of the heavy trays used to bake them, which are similar to cast iron skillets.

The dough is the other component that sets this pizza apart; it is closer to a focaccia than what's typically identified as pizza dough. The crunchy exterior crust soaked through with oil and bubbled over with caramelized cheese and an airy, light, and chewy interior crust is all thanks to these repurposed trays. The trays had edges that were slightly slanted, so when the dough cooked and the cheese melted, instead of becoming a typical Sicilian pizza, the cheese melted down the side of the crust giving the pizza a cheese crust. The corner piece all of a sudden became the most popular piece—it had a revival.

I'm partial to New York pizza—I just love it and nothing comes close in my mind. So it's even more ironic that I agreed to have Detroit-style pizza in Austin, Texas! I have to admit that I did not fall in love with this style immediately, in fact I deemed it as too thick. My taste buds still preferred NYC-style pizza. The second time I tried Detroit-style pizza was in New York and that is where I finally fell in love. I summed up my pizza love to a friend as: I wanted to marry Detroit-style pizza but have an occasional affair with greasy New York pizza.

I finally ate authentic Detroit-style pizza at its famous birthplace, Buddy's. With all of the information I gathered about the history of this pizza and what makes it so unique, I tested a few deep dish recipes and this one wins for me!

Portuguese Feijoada

4 ½ pounds pork rib rack

2 pounds pork belly

½ pound fresh lard – roughly chopped

1 linguiça link

1 large chorizo link

2 pounds white beans (such as navy beans or Boston beans)

1 pound tomatoes – diced

¾ cups olive oil

½ cup white wine (a crisp Chardonnay works well)

2 onions – diced

2 garlic cloves – finely minced

1 bay leaf

½ teaspoon ground coriander

Salt to taste

Pinch of mint leaves

1. Clean the meat and cut the rib rack into individual ribs. Rub them with salt and let rest for 1 day in the refrigerator.

2. Cook the beans as directed and reserve part of the water.

3. In a pot on medium to high heat, cook the pork belly and whole sausages in enough water to cover the meat. Once the water boils, turn the heat down and bring to a simmer for 20 minutes.

4. Remove the meats and cut the ribs and belly into small cubes. Let the meat cool down and reserve the stock.

5. In a clean pot on medium to high heat, add the olive oil with the lard.

6. When the lard melts, add the onion and garlic and stir until the onions are translucent. Add the tomatoes, coriander, and bay leaf and stir to cook until the tomato mixture separates from the oil.

7. Add the white wine and mix well. Add the reserved meat stock and cook for 5 minutes.

8. Add the beans with some of its cooking water, then add the meats and sausages. Add salt to taste.

9. Bring to a boil. Once the sauce has thickened (about 20-30 minutes), remove from heat and serve with finely chopped mint leaves sprinkled on top.

Chef Joaquim Saragga Leal serves this to his staff quite often at his restaurant Taberna Sal Grosso, so he was happy to share this recipe with me. Feijoada is a hearty Portuguese stew that will stick to your bones! I had this dish at Chef Joaquim's restaurant in Lisbon with chopped up wild boar's head, beans, and a load of picante sauce. I recommend adding a slice of bread fried in olive oil to help scoop while you eat!

Linguiça Port Reduction Grilled Cheese

For the linguiça Port sauce

2 garlic cloves – minced

1 tablespoon butter

1 cup linguiça – chopped

¼ cup red chilis – chopped*

3 cups Port wine

1 tablespoon olive oil

For the grilled cheese

Thick sandwich bread

Butter

Soft cheese such as Brie, Robiola, or Camembert – sliced**

Use malagueta peppers if you have access to them.

**In Portugal, I used Estrela de Artesanal, Queijo de Ovelha Curado.*

1. In a saucepan on medium heat, add the olive oil and garlic.
2. Add the linguiça and sauté until browned.
3. Add the red chilis and butter; stir until the butter has melted.
4. Add the Port wine. Boil until the alcohol has boiled away and the wine is reduced to half its volume.
5. Pour into a bowl and keep near.
6. Assemble the grilled cheese sandwich by first placing the cheese on top of one slice of bread.
7. Drizzle the linguiça Port sauce on the cheese, then place another slice of bread on top
8. In a flat frying pan on medium heat, melt 1 teaspoon of butter.
9. Add the sandwich to the pan and grill. Once the first side has slightly browned, flip it to brown the other side.
10. Serve once the cheese has melted.

Barrels of Port wine being trasported down the Douro River from the vineyards to the winery docks

This recipe was inspired by so many different instances in my life. I first heard about linguiça from a former colleague while talking about our ethnic backgrounds. She told me all about how her family is Portuguese and settled in Syracuse. I'll never forget the moment when I mentioned I was headed to Portugal and she immediately yelled, "OH, you have to have linguiça!" I learned all about linguiça that day–a Portuguese sausage that's high on garlic! I love it–just not on date nights.

When I visited the beautiful, majestic city of Porto in the Douro Valley of Northern Portugal, I learned all about their locally-made sweet wine called Port. Port wine is also produced elsewhere in the world, however, under strict European guidelines, only the wine produced in Portugal may be labeled as Port or Porto.

Another ingredient I use in this recipe is a pepper called malagueta. I stumbled upon these peppers at a streetside flower and herb shop while strolling the streets of Lisbon. Its rich red color and unique taste inspired me to make something truly special with it.

JAPANESE OKONOMIYAKI

1 cup flour (I like to
use whole wheat)

¾ cup dashi or water

1 egg

3 cups cabbage – shredded

1 carrot – grated

1 small zucchini – grated

1 green onion – chopped

3 bacon slices – chopped

½ cup panko

Mayonnaise to taste*

Green onions to taste – sliced

Seaweed flakes (optional)

Bonito flakes (optional)

2 tablespoons vegetable oil

For the okonomiyaki sauce

3 tablespoons ketchup

1 tablespoon
Worcestershire sauce

1 teaspoon soy sauce

1 teaspoon honey

*In Japan, the tradition is to use
Kewpie mayonnaise because of its taste
and texture. This usually can be found
in Asian grocery stores. If it cannot be
found, any brand can be used.*

1. Mix the flour, dashi/water, egg, cabbage, carrot, zucchini, and green onion in a large bowl.

2. Heat some oil in a frying pan.

3. Pour the vegetable mixture into the pan, creating a 6 inch diameter. Top with some raw bacon slices and a tablespoon of panko.

4. Cook on medium heat until golden brown on both sides, about 10 minutes per side. Repeat until the batter is finished.

5. Top with okonomiyaki sauce, mayonnaise, green onions, Bonito flakes and Seaweed flakes, if using.

Okonomiyaki, meaning "grilled as you like it", is a savory Japanese pancake made with flour, eggs, shredded cabbage, meat/protein, and topped with a variety of condiments. It's better known as *Japanese pizza* in the US. You can prepare the filling and toppings however you like it, just like the name says. This version is my favorite and a wonderful way to use up your leftovers!

Statue of Jizo along the hike up Mount Koya in Osaka.
Along with many other titles, Jizo is worshipped
as a protector of travelers. Okonomiyaki is said
to have originated in the Osaka region.

SAMURAI PORK BURGER

2 pounds ground pork

3 garlic cloves – minced

1 tablespoon
lemongrass pulp

2 cups cremini
mushrooms – quartered

1 ½ tablespoons fish sauce

1 jalapeño – seeded
and minced

1 cup cilantro
leaves – chopped

½ cup scallions – finely
chopped

6 sesame seed hamburger
buns – slit down the center

Cooking spray (such as Pam)

Pinch of black pepper

Pinch of salt

For the spread

½ cup mayonnaise

3 tablespoons lime juice

2 tablespoons peanut oil

1 tablespoon sweet
chili sauce

2 teaspoons soy sauce

1 cup cabbage shreds

¼ cup cilantro leaves on stem

1. In a mixing bowl, break apart the ground pork and set aside.

2. In a food processor, add garlic, lemongrass, mushrooms, jalapeño, scallions, fish sauce, cilantro, salt, and black pepper. Pulse until it becomes a paste.

3. Add the mushroom paste to the ground pork; mix to combine.

4. Divide into 6 patties, then refrigerate on parchment paper until ready to grill.

5. Heat your gas or charcoal grill to medium-high heat or place a non-stick grill-grated pan on the stove over medium-high heat. Spray the pan with cooking spray right before cooking.

6. Place the patties on the grill and cook for 7-8 minutes on each side, until no longer pink within.

7. While the patties are cooking, put together the spread. In a bowl, combine all of the ingredients except the cabbage. Add the cabbage last and mix well.

8. Lay down the hamburger buns and place the desired amount of slaw on each bottom bun.

9. Place the cooked pork patties inside the buns and top with more slaw.

10. Serve with a crisp cucumber salad or French fries.

I have a ritual of eating McDonald's when I travel, to try what has been tailored for the local population in each country that I visit. The Samurai Pork Burger is served in McDonald's all across Thailand. This burger stuck out, first because of its name, and secondly because of the sweet and spicy nature of each bite – just the way I like it. The recipe I've shared is my take on McDonald's version of a Thai-flavored burger.

Heavy traffic in bustling Bangkok

Local Thai tuk tuk in Bangkok

Pork, Broccoli Rabe and Provolone Subs

2 tablespoons ground fennel seeds

3 tablespoons dried parsley

1 ½ tablespoons dried thyme

1 tablespoon crushed red chili flakes, plus more to taste

1 (6-7 pounds) pork shoulder – butterflied

3 rosemary sprigs – stemmed and finely chopped

10 garlic cloves – finely chopped

4 cups beef stock

½ cup red wine

1 medium yellow onion – thinly sliced

1 bay leaf

½ cup canned crushed tomatoes

2 pounds broccoli rabe

1 pound sharp provolone – sliced

¼ cup olive oil

Crusty Italian rolls – split

Store-bought pickled cherry peppers to taste

Kosher salt and freshly ground black pepper to taste

Famous Dinic's of Reading Terminal Market in Philadelphia, Pennsylvania

1. Heat oven to 450 degrees. Combine fennel, parsley, thyme, and 3 teaspoons of chili flakes in a small bowl; set aside.

2. Open the pork shoulder on a work surface and spread with half of the herb mixture, rosemary, ¼ of the chopped garlic, salt, and pepper.

3. Roll up the pork shoulder, tie with kitchen twine at 1-inch intervals to secure, and season the outside with remaining herb mixture, salt, and pepper.

The original roast pork, provolone and broccoli rabe sub

4. Transfer to a roasting pan and roast until browned, about 40 minutes.

5. Remove pan from oven, and turn on broiler. Add remaining garlic to pan along with stock, wine, onion, and bay leaf. Pour the tomatoes over the top and sides of pork shoulder. Broil until tomatoes are caramelized, about 20 minutes.

6. Reduce oven temperature to 325 degrees, cover pork with parchment paper, and cover roasting pan with aluminum foil. Cook for about 2 hours. Remove from the oven and set aside to cool completely.

7. Transfer pork to a cutting board, remove the bay leaf from the pan and transfer juices to a blender to puree.

8. Add the puree to a large saucepan and keep warm.

9. Pull pork apart into large pieces and add to saucepan with the puree.

10. Meanwhile, bring a large pot of salted water to a boil and add the broccoli rabe. Cook, stirring until just tender, 2-3 minutes.

11. Drain and transfer to a bowl of ice water to cool. Drain, then dry thoroughly with paper towels.

12. Heat oil in a 12-inch skillet and add remaining chili flakes and broccoli rabe. Cook, stirring until crisp and warmed through, about 4 minutes. Set aside.

13. Place 4 slices of provolone on the bottom half of each roll and top with pork. Add broccoli rabe and peppers.

This sandwich is the lesser known obsession of local Philly dwellers just after the famous cheesesteak. There is a popular place in Reading Terminal Market called DiNic's where sandwich lovers wait in line, sometimes for over an hour, to get their original version of a pork, broccoli rabe and provolone sub. Making this at home will take your taste buds on a trip to Philly, without the wait!

PORTUGUESE FRANCESINHA

8 thick slices white bread

2 tablespoons butter

¼ pound thinly sliced ham

¼ pound cooked chorizo–sliced

¼ pound Portuguese linguiça
sausage–sliced

12 slices good-quality cheddar cheese

¼ cooked sirloin steak–sliced (optional)

¼ pound Cooked chipolatas–halved
lengthways (optional)

Francesinha sauce

2 tablespoons butter

1 ½ cups beef stock

1 small carrot–grated

1 small onion–grated

2 tablespoons tomato paste

1 bay leaf

¼ cup Port or whisky

2 cups lager or light ale

½ cup milk

1 tablespoon cornflour mixed
with 2 tablespoons cold water

1 tablespoon piri-piri sauce, Tabasco
or ½ teaspoon chili powder

½ teaspoon salt

1. To make the Francesinha sauce, heat the butter in a medium-sized saucepan over high heat and add the carrot, onion, and salt. Cook, stirring regularly for 5 minutes, until the vegetables are caramelized and fragrant.

2. Add the tomato paste, stir for a minute, then add the bay leaf, Port, beer, beef stock, and milk; bring to a boil.

3. Reduce the heat and simmer for 30 minutes.

4. Stir in the cornflour and piri-piri (if using) until the sauce has thickened. Add less piri-piri or chili if you want the sauce less spicy.

5. The sauce should be the consistency of thin gravy. Strain the sauce to remove any solids, adjust the seasoning, and keep hot until ready to serve.

6. For the sandwich, toast the bread and butter it lightly. Preheat oven to 375 degrees.

7. Top the toast with a layer of each type of meat, then add another slice of bread.

8. Lay the cheese slices over the top slice of bread so they hang over the sides of the sandwich.

9. Bake the sandwich so the melted cheese wraps around the bread.

10. To serve, pour the hot Francesinha sauce over the sandwich or serve the sauce on the side in a small jug to use as desired.

I tasted this meaty sandwich in Porto and after eating it with a side of French fries and a cold beer, I was stuffed!

Francesinha is Porto's iconic sandwich that has a French cousin, the Croque Madame. The clue is in Francesinha's name, literally translating to "little Frenchie". In the 1950s and 1960s, António Salazar's harsh dictatorship turned millions of Portuguese into migrants. By 1970, when the population of Lisbon numbered barely 800,000, at least 700,000 of them were living in France. As well as money, the migrants sent elements of French culture home to Portugal, the Croque Monsieur being one of them, which the Portuguese took to their hearts. The classic French grilled cheese sandwich was adapted and the meagre Croque Monsieur became the Francesinha – no longer a moder-ate-sized snack, but a big, strong meal and a force to be reckoned with. Francesinha is a chef favorite in Portugal!

David da Silva, who was working at Restaurante A Regaleira in Porto, became known for his kitchen experiments and inspired cooking. While in France, he fell in love with the attitude of French women and decided to play with the recipe for Croque Madame to add a few extra ingredients that would combine what he liked about both Portuguese and French women through the dish – the boldness of Portuguese women and the essence of French women – ultimately creating a dish that was less conventional with a touch of spice. He added grilled pork, linguiça (smoke-cured pork sausage) and sausage, between two slabs of bread, covered by melted cheese and immersed in a spicy beer and tomato sauce, often topped with a fried egg and surrounded by chips. His creation was recently considered one of the 10 best sandwiches in the world by certain media giants.

The Francesinha is regarded as a snack, which used to be served after hours when groups of friends gathered to have a bite to eat late at night. Its social vocation has not been lost; "To eat a Francesinha" is still a pretext to catch up with friends around a table. Locals say, "The Francesinha is more than a recipe; it is socializing in the Porto way."

BANH XEO

Savory Vietnamese crepes stuffed with shrimp, pork belly and mushrooms!

For the batter

3 cups + 4 tablespoons rice flour

¼ teaspoon turmeric

¼ teaspoon cumin

½ teaspoon sugar

2 ¾ cups water

½ teaspoon salt

1 tablespoon vegetable oil

For the filling

1 shallot – peeled

1 cup cremini mushrooms

1 teaspoon sesame oil

½ Thai chili – chopped

1 medium garlic clove

1 teaspoon ginger – peeled and finely grated

1 teaspoon ketchup

1 tablespoon fish sauce

1 teaspoon light soy sauce

½ pound small shrimp – peeled and deveined

½ pound pork belly – thinly sliced

2 tablespoons garlic chives – sliced

1 cup bean sprouts

For the nuoc cham (dipping sauce)

4 tablespoons water

2 tablespoons sugar

1 tablespoon lime juice

2 tablespoons fish sauce

1 Thai chili – sliced (use more or less for heat)

½ teaspoon grated garlic

Garnishes

Thai basil

Red leaf lettuce

Mint

Cilantro

Grilled bok choy (optional)

1. To make the nuoc cham (dipping sauce), in a small bowl, mix all ingredients until well incorporated. Refrigerate until ready to use.

2. To make the batter, in a large bowl, combine all ingredients except oil, allow mixture to sit for at least an hour refrigerated and up to 6 hours.

3. To make the filling, place everything but the shrimp, pork belly, mushrooms, and bean sprouts in a food processor and blend until smooth. Add shrimp and lightly pulse until combined.

4. Heat a large non-stick sauté pan and cook pork belly until crispy; remove and set aside.

5. In the same pan, add mushrooms and cook until the water has evaporated. Add the shrimp mixture on high heat and cook until shrimp is just pink in color.

6. Add bean sprouts, season with salt, and stir. Remove and set aside. Wipe out the pan with a paper towel.

7. In the same pan, drizzle vegetable oil. Just before the oil reaches the smoking point, pour the cold batter into the pan, swirling it so the batter edges reach the outer "corners" of the pan. Turn the heat down to medium-low.

8. Sprinkle the crispy pork belly and the shrimp & mushroom mixture onto one side of the crepe. Cover the pan with a lid or plate. Allow to cook for 2-3 minutes until done.

9. Add desired garnishes, fold crepe in half, cut into wedges and serve with the nuoc cham dipping sauce.

Dip each rolled wrapper into nuoc cham to get a sweet and spicy flavor blast!

"Sufi Spice Bazaar" – Sevgi Uca, Istanbul, Turkey

MEAT

LAHMACUN – TURKISH PIZZA

1 medium onion – finely chopped or grated

2 medium tomatoes – finely chopped

1 bunch flat leaf parsley – finely chopped

8 ounces lean ground lamb

1 tablespoon tomato paste

1 teaspoon paprika flakes (or pul biber), plus more if you like spice

1 tablespoon lemon juice

6 round pre-made Indian naan or flour tortillas (depending on how thick you want the crust – I use tortillas)

1 tablespoon olive oil

Salt and ground black pepper to taste

1. In a frying pan on medium heat, sauté the onions in olive oil until translucent.

2. Add the chopped tomatoes and cook until the tomatoes become a chunky paste. Add salt to taste and set aside to cool.

3. In a large bowl, combine the ground lamb, tomato paste, parsley, paprika flakes, lemon juice, cooked onions, and tomatoes; season with salt and pepper. Work this mixture into a paste with your hands or a wooden spoon.

4. Cover and keep in the refrigerator until you are ready to use.

5. Oil 1-2 baking sheets and place the naan or tortillas on them.

6. Spread a thin layer of the meat mixture on top of the bread, covering the edges too.

7. Bake in the oven for about 15 minutes, until the meat is nicely cooked.

Serve Lahmacun hot with lemon wedges and sumac on the side. I also add chopped raw onions and more parsley on top of mine.

Lahmacun in Turkey

Diners enjoying a night out of delicious food on a narrow path behind Istiklal Avenue known as Nevizade Restaurants Road, Istanbul's most vibrant eating destination

AUSTRALIAN MEAT PIE ROLLS

1 pound beef – minced or cut into fine pieces

2 ounces bacon – finely chopped

2 tablespoons butter

1 large onion – finely chopped

½ cup red wine

1 ½ tablespoons Vegemite

1 tablespoon cornstarch

1 tablespoon water

½ bunch parsley – finely chopped

2 pinches grated nutmeg

1 egg yolk

1 tablespoon milk

1 package frozen puff pastry – thawed

Freshly ground pepper

Salt

1. To make the meat filling, place a large frying pan on medium heat. Fry the bacon, then remove the pieces from the pan.

2. Add the onions to the bacon grease and sauté until translucent. Return the bacon pieces to the pan, add the beef, and sauté until brown.

3. Deglaze the pan with the red wine and add the Vegemite. Stir well, then turn the heat to low, cover, and simmer for 1 hour.

4. Dissolve the cornstarch in the tablespoon of water, then add it to the meat. Add the parsley, nutmeg, and salt and pepper to taste. Keep in mind that Vegemite and bacon already add a salty element.

5. Cook for a few more minutes, then remove from the heat. Allow the meat to cool completely.

6. Preheat oven to 425 degrees.

7. Unfold the puff pastry dough onto a lightly floured surface; you should have 2 big squares. Cut each square in half so that you have 4 long rectangles.

8. Divide the meat mixture into 4 equal parts and spoon a long line of meat down each rectangle.

Sydney Opera House in the harbor

9. Roll the pastry up and over the sausage, then pinch the seams of dough together so that you have four long logs. Cut each log into four sections then place the sections on a cookie sheet or baking pan lined with parchment paper.

10. Whisk the egg yolk with milk and brush each roll with the egg mixture.

11. Bake at 425 degrees for only 5 minutes; reduce the heat to 350 degrees and bake 30-35 more minutes.

12. Remove each roll from the pan and allow to cool on top of paper towels.

In Australia, meat pies have a culture of their own, with variations as unique as Thai curry pies. A popular pie chain in Sydney called Pie Face serves up all types of meat pies imaginable, along with their signature drawing of a smiley face on top of the pie crust. A meat pie can be eaten on the go, if a smaller portion is purchased, or as part of a plated meal with greens. Another popular "on the go" favorite in the Land Down Under are sausage rolls. I combined these two favorites by creating a meat pie filling and putting it into a sausage roll pastry. Australian meat pies and sausage rolls are traditionally eaten as is or dipped into ketchup.

PICA PAU

2 pounds flank/rump steak

4-5 garlic cloves – minced

2 cups white wine

2 ounces butter

1 bay leaf

2 teaspoons salt

1 teaspoon black pepper

1 cup pickled vegetables

Pica Pau at Taberna Sal Grossa in Lisbon, Portugal

1. Season the steak liberally with salt and pepper.

2. In a frying pan on medium to high heat, add 1 tablespoon of butter and cook the steak to desired doneness. Remove the steak and set aside to rest.

3. Meanwhile, add the remaining butter, garlic, bay leaf, and white wine and sauté until the garlic becomes soft, about 5 minutes. Remove from heat and set aside.

4. Slice the steak, pour over the sauce, top with pickles, and serve with toothpicks to eat!

Pica Pau is a simple and delicious Portuguese recipe provided by Chef Joaquim Saragga Leal, chef and owner of Taberna Sal Grosso in Lisbon, Portugal. I tried this dish at one of the various food markets scattered all over Lisbon and liked the tartness of the pickles paired with a meaty steak. It was a fun and communal experience to eat this dish with toothpicks along with a glass of wine.

The tabernas in Portugal have an uncomparable rustic charm

STEAK PINCHITOS

1 pound chuck steak–large cubes

2 tablespoons pinchito spice blend

2 tablespoons olive oil

For the pinchito spice blend

2 teaspoons sugar

1 tablespoon paprika

1 teaspoon black pepper

1 tablespoon cumin

1 tablespoon thyme

2 teaspoons salt

Tools

Wooden/Bamboo skewers–soaked in water for at least 2 hours

1. In a large mixing bowl, combine 1 tablespoon of olive oil and the spice blend; mix well.

2. Add the steak and mix enough to coat all of the meat.

3. Marinate for at least 1 hour in the refrigerator.

4. Thread the steak on the skewers, bunching the meat closely together.

5. In a large, flat pan on medium heat, add the other tablespoon of olive oil. Carefully place each skewer in the pan.

6. When the steak has browned on one side, flip each skewer and continue cooking on the other side until browned. Alternatively, bake the skewers for 20 minutes in a 375 degree oven.

7. Remove the steak from the pan, plate and enjoy!

I discovered Pinchitos in Spain where they're a prevalent "meat on a stick". Native to the Andalusian region of Spain, Pinchitos are typically any type of meat or seafood flavored with spices that almost always include paprika. Due to its close proximity to Northern Africa, Andalusian cuisine is highly influenced by techniques and flavors common to the Moors, a population of Muslim inhabitants from Northwestern Africa. Similar dishes with different flavors exist in Greece with Souvlaki, Japan with Yakitori, and the Island of Madeira in Portugal with Espetada.

Different types of pimenton spice sold at Valencia's Central Market in Spain

PHILLY CHEESESTEAK SAMOSA

1 package phyllo pastry

1 pound ground beef

1 onion – thinly sliced

1 bell pepper – thinly sliced

1 cup mushrooms
(optional) – finely chopped

¼ hot pickled cherry
peppers – finely chopped

1 cup Cheez Whiz

2 tablespoons olive oil

Salt and pepper to taste

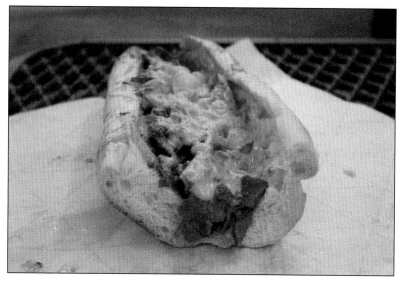

The original cheesesteak from Pat's King of Steaks in Philadelphia, Pennsylvania

1. Pour 1 tablespoon of olive oil in a frying pan and brown the beef on high heat.

2. Once browned, add the mushrooms (if using), bell peppers, onions, and cherry peppers.

3. Season with salt and pepper, and stir until the onions become slightly translucent. Remove from the heat.

4. Preheat oven to 350 degrees and place one sheet of phyllo pastry on a work surface. Brush lightly with olive oil. Fold into half lengthwise.

5. Place 1½ to 2 tablespoons of filling in one corner. Fold the pastry corner over the filling to create a triangle. Continue folding until the entire strip of pastry is used and a triangular parcel is formed. Repeat with remaining phyllo pastry until all filling is used.

6. Place the pastry parcels seam-side down on a lightly-oiled baking tray and lightly brush the tops with oil.

7. Bake for about 30 minutes or until golden brown.

8. Heat the Cheez Whiz per its packaging instructions and serve with the cheesesteak samosas for dipping.

BALKAN GOULASH

1 yellow onion – chopped

1 pound tender chuck steak – cubed

3 tablespoons paprika

½ teaspoon pepper

2 celery sticks – chopped

2 large carrots – chopped

1 cup fingerling potatoes or chopped potatoes

½ teaspoon salt

2 tablespoons olive oil

Traditional Goulash being cooked over a handmade coal fire in Croatia

1. Heat the olive oil in a pan over medium heat. Top with the onions and then the beef. Do not mix it and let it simmer for 15-20 minutes.

2. Add the paprika, salt, and pepper. Simmer for another 5 minutes.

3. Add the chopped carrots and celery. Now mix and simmer for another 5 minutes.

4. Add the potatoes and 2 cups of water. Simmer on low for 30-40 minutes. Add water as it evaporates, or less if you prefer a thicker sauce.

I had Goulash in Croatia where the stew is quite common to find in restaurants and in local homes, though its roots are in Hungary. It's a hearty and meaty dish with simple ingredients. Serve with a loaf of bread and don't be shy dipping the bread into the Goulash. This dish pairs best with an intense red wine like Merlot.

FRENCH BASQUE AXOA

**2 pounds veal/beef/
turkey – ground**

**4 tablespoons duck
fat (or butter)**

¾ cups dry white wine

½ small onion – thinly sliced

4 garlic cloves – chopped

**1 teaspoon Piment
d'Espelette powder (or
chopped jalapeños)**

**3 red bell peppers – roasted,
peeled, and seeded**

1 teaspoon beef bouillon

3 tablespoons olive oil

Salt to taste

1. In a skillet, heat the oil over medium heat, then add the onion and garlic.

2. Add the duck fat or butter and brown the meat in the skillet.

3. Add a pinch of the Espelette pepper powder (or jalapeños), roasted peppers, and a little salt. Stir for 10 minutes.

4. Add the white wine, beef bouillon and enough water to completely cover the ingredients without drowning them. Stir this mixture until it is combined.

5. Reduce heat if necessary and stew for about 40 minutes.

6. Uncover and stir, there should be a little bit of jus left. Add salt to taste.

The Basque region is the only place in France that really cooks with Piment d'Espelette, and Piment d'Espelette is the only spice in France with an AOC. An AOC is a seal that is given to certain native French products which ensures those products cannot be sold or manufactured outside of a specific region. This particular pepper combines a slight spiciness similar to that of a jalapeño with a deep sweetness similar to that of roasted red bell peppers – these are also your substitutes if you can't find Espelette pepper for this recipe.

In French Basque country, locals dry the pepper by hanging them on strings outside their homes and once dried this pepper is used in just about anything. It's added to soups, used as a grilling marinade, and even added to desserts! What amazed me when I first tried this stew was how much it reminded me of a Texan chili, but with a surprisingly lighter feel. Axoa is traditionally eaten with stewed potatoes or rice and a glass of red wine, but my favorite way to eat it is with toasted French bread and a crisp beer.

Turkish Manti

For the manti

1 package wonton wrappers

1 egg–beaten

8 ounces lean ground beef (or ground lamb)

1 onion–grated or very finely chopped

Salt and freshly ground black pepper to taste

For the garlic yogurt

2 ¼ cups creamy plain yogurt

2 garlic cloves–minced

1 tablespoon butter

Salt to taste

For the sauce

1 tablespoon Turkish hot pepper paste, biber salcasi or tomato paste

2 teaspoons dried mint

1 teaspoon ground sumac (optional)

1 teaspoon Turkish red pepper flakes, pul biber or chili flakes

4 tablespoons olive oil

1. In a medium-sized bowl, combine the onion with the ground meat, season with salt and ground black pepper, and mix well.

2. Lay out 8 wonton wrappers and brush each one with egg wash.

3. Place ½ tablespoon of the meat (or more if you want) in the center of each wrapper, then top each mound of meat with another wrapper; press down on the edges. Repeat until you run out of meat. Use a ravioli cutter to form shapes, if desired.

4. Add water and a pinch of salt to a large pot and bring to a boil.

5. Gently place the dumplings into the boiling water and simmer for about 2-3 minutes, until they are cooked.

6. Once cooked, drain the water and place the manti in a serving dish. Drizzle a little oil over them so that they don't stick together.

7. In a separate bowl, beat the yogurt with the garlic and season with salt to your taste.

8. In a large skillet, add the butter and melt on medium heat. Add the yogurt mixture and cook the yogurt for 5-10 minutes.

9. To prepare the red sauce, heat the oil in a wide pan and add the biber salcasi or the tomato paste. Stir in the red pepper flakes or pul biber, dried mint, and sumac; combine well and simmer for 1-2 minutes.

10. To serve, spoon the garlic yogurt over the manti, then the red pepper paste sauce over the garlic yogurt. You can decorate with extra red pepper flakes, dried mint, and sumac. Serve immediately.

The use of yogurt is really prevalent in Turkish cuisine. Yogurt is considered *The Mother of Dairy* in Turkey. It is used in desserts, savory dishes, drinks, and just about anything edible. Eggs are even poached in yogurt! Turkey has a yogurt drink that is very similar to Indian Lassi called Ayran that I have tried at both Turkish and Lebanese eateries many times. You need to try this recipe for Ayran:

1 cup yogurt

1 cup cold water

Salt to taste

Method: Mix everything with a hand blender until smooth.

I knew I would try a lot of dips and maybe even desserts with yogurt, but I didn't think I would have tiny dumplings with a yogurt sauce ladled on top instead of a tomato or herb-based sauce. Manti is an extraordinary dish that is one of those all-time homey comfort dishes in Turkey.

These delicious tiny treasures of dumplings stuffed with spiced meat and topped with a yogurt garlic based sauce and a spicy oil is an odd combination at first glance but, once you taste it you see how the combination works surprisingly well. That's exactly what happened to me.

I was so hungry when I arrived to Istanbul late at night, so I opened the 24-hour room service menu and saw "Manti – Traditional Turkish Dumplings". I thought, well that sounds like comfort food, so I ordered it. When the plate arrived and I lifted the silver cover, I saw the yogurt underneath a spicy red oil and freaked out a little bit because I was so hungry and it wasn't a combination I had seen before. I wanted something familiar after a long flight with an even longer layover. Since it was there though, I tried a bite and to my surprise, it all worked. The yogurt wasn't tart like I expected; instead it was a creamy, garlicky sauce with just the right amount of spice from the oil.

When I visited the Spice Bazaar a few days later, I spent the entire day browsing and inevitably asked about the various dishes I had tried up until that point. From the conversations I had that day, I slowly put this recipe together.

ĆEVAPČIĆI

1 ½ pounds ground pork

1 pound lean ground beef

½ pound ground lamb

1 egg white

4 garlic cloves – minced

1 teaspoon baking soda

2 teaspoons ground black pepper

½ teaspoon paprika

1 teaspoon salt

1 tablespoon olive oil

1. Preheat a grill to medium-low heat or preheat oven to 350 degrees.

2. In a large bowl, combine all of the ingredients except for the olive oil.

3. Using your hands, form the meat mixture into finger length sausages ¾-inch thick.

4. Lightly oil the grill surface or foil-lined baking pan.

5. Place the sausages on the grill or in the baking dish and grill until cooked through, about 30 minutes.

6. If grilling, turn the sausages as needed. If baking, turn the sausages after 15 minutes of baking in the oven.

Diocletan's Palace in Split, Croatia

Diocletian's Palace in Split, Croatia is one of the most impressive surviving Roman ruins on the Adriatic Coast. Emperor Diocletian built the palace perhaps as a retirement home after giving up his throne in the 4th century. The emperor built the palace as his playground, outfitted with a palace-side ship dock so he could come and go straight from the palace steps. The palace was made from local limestone and marble and took up approximately 8 acres. Today the remains of the palace structure include the original walls and gates and certain antiques such as a 3,500 year old sphinx that was gifted to the emperor from Egypt.

The palace is particularly beautiful to see at night as the walls and columns are illuminated to have a fairytale effect against the deep blue night sky. It is the center of the city and houses restaurants, bars, local shops and so on.

When you're having a night out in Diocletian's Palace and 1 a.m. hits, everyone flocks to a spot that serves an iconic dish, Ćevapčići. It is a Balkan skinless meat sausage that is served in a split flatbread spread with copious amounts of Ajvar (p. 2) and topped with chopped onions. It's a late night snack that you will keep thinking about, especially at 1 a.m.!

BOEUF BOURGUIGNON

8 ounces pancetta – diced

3 pounds boneless short ribs*

1 large carrot – chopped

1 onion – chopped

2 tablespoons flour

¾ bottle red wine – full-bodied
like Bordeaux or Burgundy

3 cups beef stock

1 tablespoon tomato paste

2 garlic cloves

2 thyme sprigs

2 bay leaves

¼ teaspoon crushed black pepper

1 teaspoon salt, adjust to taste

1 tablespoon olive oil

For the braised onions and mushrooms

2 tablespoons butter

2 tablespoons olive oil

16 ounces frozen pearl onions – defrosted

1 pound cremini mushrooms – quartered

1 cup beef stock

1 bay leaf

1 thyme sprig

1 tablespoon parsley – chopped

Other stewing meats work too, but I prefer short ribs that fall apart after stewing.

1. Preheat oven to 325 degrees.

2. Pour the tablespoon of olive oil into a large dutch oven on medium heat.

3. Add the pancetta and sauté until it begins to brown, about 2-3 minutes. Remove the pancetta with a slotted spoon and place into a side dish.

4. In the same pot, add the beef a few pieces at a time and brown on all sides. Remove the beef with a slotted spoon and set aside. Repeat until all beef pieces are browned.

5. In the same pot, sauté the onions and carrots until the onions are translucent and carrots have softened. Add back the beef and pancetta. Add in salt, black pepper, flour and stir all of the content until the flour coats the beef pieces.

6. Continue stirring for another 5 minutes and then add in the wine and stock. The beef should be slightly visible.

7. Add in tomato paste, garlic, and herbs.

8. Bring the stew to a simmer on the stove and then cover the dutch oven and place in the oven. Cook in the oven slowly for at least 4 hours.

9. The meat will be done when it can fall apart once pierced with a fork.

10. While the meat is cooking, prepare the onion and mushroom sauce.

11. In a large skillet, add all of the butter and oil on medium heat and add in mushrooms.

12. Sauté the mushrooms for until they are soft, about 5 minutes. Remove for the skillet and set aside.

13. Add in onions and roll around on the pan so they become evenly browned, about 10 minutes.

14. Pour in stock, add salt, pepper, and all of the herbs. Cook until the stock has a light simmer.

15. Add in mushrooms and continue to simmer for another 10 minutes.

16. Once the meat is done, remove from the oven, stir and place in serving dishes. Top with onion and mushroom mixture.

This tastes best with mashed potatoes or mashed cauliflower! I also add a few drops of black truffle oil and/or shavings to enhance the mushroom flavors–you won't regret it!

The first time I ever heard of Boeuf Bourguignon was in Julie and Julia, a movie featuring a young New Yorker's pursuit of mastering Julia Child's French recipes. After watching the scene where Julie burns the Boeuf and immediately has a breakdown, I was both curious and intimidated. Before watching the movie, when I went to French restaurants such as Pastis or Brasserie Les Halles in New York, I would just stick to croque monsieur or escargot and wouldn't venture further.

A few years ago, a corporate colleague and I were working on a project very late one night. We were working with a large set of data and needed to get the data into a presentable graphic for executive management that would "tell the story". It was around 10 p.m. and we finally got it to work! We wanted to celebrate with food and drinks. My colleague, an Italian from Milan, suggested a place by the seaport called Stella on Front Street since he knew the bartender—perfect for me since it was close to my apartment.

Stella is an old school bar/restaurant with a menu that has European flare and Wall Street hot shot clientele. We ordered some vino (keeping it classy and elegant), I chose polenta with a meat ragout, and my colleague decided on the Boeuf Bourguignon. We shared and it was absolutely delicious. Unfortunately, Stella closed down due to Hurricane Sandy damage.

Cut to the holiday season in 2010. I went to London to visit family around Christmas and my closest cousin and I planned a 5-day trip to Paris for New Years. I was so amped to visit Paris for the first time. From what I had heard and seen in movies, Paris seemed like such a beautiful city and a gastronomical adventure. I definitely wanted to visit some of the best restaurants in Paris (and in the world quite frankly). My list included L'Atelier by Joel Robuchon, the super trendy and amazing experience at Buddha Bar, Laduree and Brasserie Bofinger.

L'Atelier is one of the hardest reservations to get as it only has about 15 seats around their beautiful open air kitchen. Luckily we were able to score reservations for lunch which was just perfect. We sat down, started with champagne, had a few appetizers, and then it was time to order our mains. After my various introductions to the dish over the years, I just HAD to order the Boeuf Bourguignon, and oh.my.god. it was worth every Euro and calorie. My cousin even confessed that she also dreams of that dish sometimes! They made it with beef cheek, a robust red wine, aromatics, tons of butter and braised it for hours... simply divine!

Since that experience in Paris, I have made Boeuf Bourguignon numerous times, making changes here and there until I finally perfected it! Basically, I braise short ribs for hours with a really good red wine from the Burgundy region of France, mirepoix, aromatics, and beef stock. I also add another ingredient which blows this dish out of the roof... truffle shavings!

The unique countryside
in Burgundy, France

LAMB CHOPS WITH MUSHROOM SAUCE

For the lamb marinade

8 lamb rib chops

1 teaspoon chili powder

3 tablespoons almond meal

1 inch ginger – chopped

8 garlic cloves – chopped

3 green chilis – chopped

1 small papaya – peeled,
seeded, and chopped
(or ⅔ cup of organic
papaya concentrate)

1 teaspoon garam masala

2 teaspoons MDH
Meat Masala*

3 teaspoons olive oilJ

uice of one lime

Salt to taste

For the mushroom sauce

8 ounces portabella
mushrooms – chopped

½ cup organic chicken broth

1 teaspoon olive oil

1 teaspoon MDH Meat
Masala (optional)

Salt to taste

*This can be found in South Asian
grocery stores.*

1. To marinate the lamb chops, wash the chops and place them in a vessel deep enough to allow the marinade to cover all of the chops.

2. Marinate the chops in the lime juice, chili powder and a pinch of salt while you make the rest of the marinade.

3. Heat 1 teaspoon of the oil in a small saucepan. Add the almond meal, stirring continuously for 1-2 minutes until the flour forms a smooth sandy paste and you begin to smell a nutty aroma. Transfer the paste to a bowl and leave to cool.

4. Blend the remaining marinade ingredients into a smooth paste using a food processor or a blender. Spread both pastes over the marinated meat and refrigerate for a minimum of 4 hours. For the best results, marinate lamb chops overnight.

5. When ready to cook the chops, add 1 teaspoon of olive oil into a cast iron skillet over medium heat.

6. Preheat oven to 400 degrees.

7. Remove the lamb chops from the marinade one by one and place each in the cast iron skillet. Reserve the marinade to use for cooking the mushroom sauce. Cook chops for 2-3 minutes on each side, until both sides are brown and starting to char.

8. When all lamb chops have browned, place the cast iron skillet in the preheated oven for 10 minutes to complete cooking them.

9. While the chops are cooking, add 1 teaspoon of olive oil to a nonstick pan over medium heat and add the mushrooms.

10. Sauté the mushrooms for 1 minute. Add the marinade sauce and stir for another 2 minutes.

11. Add the chicken broth, then allow the sauce to cook down until your desired consistency.

12. Add salt to taste and the optional MDH Meat Masala to reach your desired amount of seasoning.

I am a huge lover of lamb chops! At Middle Eastern, Greek, and especially Indian restaurants, if there are lamb chops on the menu, I will order them without a doubt. When I was in Rajasthan, India I ate the best lamb chops I have ever tasted at Jai Mahal Palace, a palace converted into a 5-star hotel. They were succulent, extremely flavorful, and had a little crust which added to the umami tsunami going on in my mouth.

My modus operandi when I eat around the world is to speak to the chefs behind the dishes I fall head over heels for so that I can pry the secret ingredients out of him/her or tell them my thoughts on the dish. In this instance, the head chef was a cool guy (no prying needed) and explained to me that marinating the lamb in papaya puree and spices overnight will tenderize the meat to an exceptional level.

Serve the lamb chops with the mushroom sauce drizzled on top and a side of mashed sweet potatoes. The little crunch given by the almond meal is one of my favorite parts while eating these chops–enjoy!

MONTREAL SMOKED MEAT SANDWICHES

5 pounds beef brisket

For the brine

16 cups water

6 ounces sugar

2 ounces dark brown sugar

2 ounces honey

8 garlic cloves–minced

1 tablespoon store-bought pickling spice*

6 ounces sea salt

2 ounces hickory smoked sea salt

For the spice crust

¾ cup black peppercorns

⅓ cup coriander seeds

⅓ cup mustard seeds

1 tablespoon store-bought pickling spice*

⅛ cup hickory smoked sea salt

For the pickling spice (optional)

In a spice grinder, grind together
1 tablespoon each of:

black peppercorns

mustard seeds

coriander seeds

hot red pepper flakes

allspice berries

whole cloves

ground ginger powder

ground mace powder

cinnamon powder

crumbled bay leaves

Local supermarkets sell spice jars of pre-mixed pickling spices that work well for this recipe. However, if you'd like to create your own magic, then try my quick recipe below.

Plan ahead for this recipe. The meat will need to sit in the brine for at least 48 hours prior to cooking.

1. Place a large saucepan, big enough to hold 16 cups of water, on medium heat and pour in the water.

2. Add all of the brine ingredients and bring to a simmer. Continue stirring until the salt and sugar have completely dissolved, then turn off the heat. Let the brine cool completely to room temperature.

3. When cool, submerge the brisket inside the brine. Cover the brisket with a plate and press it down to ensure the meat stays submerged, then cover the pot as well. Place it in the refrigerator to allow the meat to brine for at least 48 hours, and up to 72 hours.

4. Preheat oven to 220 degrees.

5. To make the spice grind, toast the coriander and mustard seeds in a pan on medium heat until the seeds start popping rapidly. Remove the seeds from the pan and grind them using a mortar and pestle or a spice grinder; pour the mixture into a bowl.

6. Grind the black peppercorns with the pickling spice mix and add them to the ground coriander and mustard seeds. Add the hickory smoked sea salt and mix well. Set the spice mixture aside.

7. Rinse the brisket under water and pat it dry. Place the meat on top of 2 sheets of heavy-duty aluminum foil and apply a generous coat of the spice crust mixture on all sides; the mixture should stick to the meat.

8. Wrap the meat with the foil, then cut slits on the bottom side of the foil to drain excess liquid. Place the packet on a baking rack over a roasting pan.

9. Place the meat in the oven and allow it to cook for 12 hours.

10. After 12 hours, turn off the oven and allow the meat to cool inside the oven for another hour.

To serve, remove the brisket from the foil, slice, sprinkle with a pinch of hickory smoked salt, and serve on rye bread smeared with mustard.

Smoked meat sandwich at Shwartz's in Montreal, Canada

The colorful homes of the famous Avenue Henri Julien in Montreal, Canada

I went to have lunch at Mile End in Brooklyn when it first opened and it took me back to the first time I had a Montreal-style smoked meat sandwich from Schwartz's Deli.

I come from a huge, globally-spread Punjabi family which means there are always events, parties, babies being born, weddings, housewarmings, birthday parties...you get the point—there's always something to celebrate.

During New Years in 2009, my family was invited to a cousin's wedding in Montreal. I had already maxed out my vacation days at the office so I couldn't take much time off to join my family's road trip up there. I'm not overly fond of road trips anyways, especially if I've driven the road before, which we had done when I was a teen. Instead, I had heard of a beautiful train route from NYC to Montreal which travels through Vermont.

It was an unbelievably scenic train ride and the snow fall made it look magical! I arrived in Montreal, was picked up by family, and the craziness involved in Punjabi weddings immediately began! I had never met some of the family members attending and others I hadn't seen for years. The questions and comments started... How old are you? Where do you live? Oh wow near Wall Street. *Inni gori haigi* (so fair skinned). Do you speak Hindi? It's your turn next, *chai beta* (tea, my child)? *Puttar kithe Ja rahi ho* (where are you going)?

It was a hilarious experience and especially unique that when everyone was together there were four languages being spoken in the room at one time including English, Punjabi, Hindi, and French (my cousins and their friends speak French).

The food! Punjabi weddings are known for good food and not only at the actual wedding functions, but also in the homes of the people hosting. Food is one of the highlights of these events and it's plentiful. I was surrounded by makhanis, tandoori this, achari that, puris, chole, paneer in many forms, chicken, lamb, seafood, biryanis... basically overloaded with Indian masala.

With the fickle palate that I have that's constantly seeking change like a commitment-phobe boyfriend, by the second day I needed something different to nosh on. As everyone was chowing down on the Indian khana "food" in Hindi, one of my uncles walked in with a huge tray of something, walked over to me, and said, "I want you to try this... it's a Montreal thing."

He made me a sandwich of smoked meat from a landmark deli called Schwartz's Deli. It's spiced meat, cured for days and smoked for hours on rye bread with mustard and sour pickle. OH MY GOD! I was in heaven! It was like the whole room went a blur as my sandwich and I had a moment! I was absolutely loving Montreal. Words do not do this meat justice... it's the best sandwich I've ever had! In fact, the next year when my cousin came to visit me from Montreal, he called and asked if I wanted him to bring anything and I said, "SMOKED MEAT!" He successfully smuggled some over the Canadian border for me.

I haven't been to Montreal since 2009 and have been making do with the occasional visit to Katz's in the city (NYC's landmark meat joint), but in my mind it doesn't hold a match to the Schwartz's in Montreal.

One winter in my NYC apartment, I decided I wanted to make it. I went to multiple Jewish delis asking all sorts of people how they made it in their family, if they did. I took mental notes during every conversation and finally tried making it at home. After just the second try, I knew I had my recipe and a way to hold myself over until future trips to Montreal!

JAMAICAN CURRY GOAT

For the curry powder

5 tablespoons ground turmeric

4 tablespoons coriander seeds

3 tablespoons cayenne pepper

1 tablespoon ground ginger

1 tablespoon grated nutmeg

1 tablespoon whole allspice

3 tablespoons fenugreek seeds

2 tablespoons cumin seeds

2 tablespoons whole black pepper

2 tablespoons star anise

2 tablespoons yellow mustard seeds

1 tablespoon whole cloves

For the curry goat

3 pounds goat meat – chopped into cubes

1 teaspoon black pepper

6 tablespoons curry powder

1 large yellow onion – sliced

1 large yellow onion – diced

6 garlic cloves – minced

1 Scotch bonnet pepper – sliced with seeds discarded

1 thyme sprig

1 tablespoon tomato paste

2 cups boiling water

2 teaspoons salt

4 tablespoons olive oil

1. Place all of the curry powder ingredients in a spice grinder and grind until a powder is formed.

2. In a large bowl, combine the 1 tablespoon oil, curry powder mix with the goat meat, salt, black pepper, sliced onions, garlic, and Scotch bonnet peppers. Marinate the meat in the refrigerator overnight or for at least 5 hours.

3. Place a large saucepan or cast iron pot on high heat and add remaining oil.

4. Carefully place each piece of meat into the pan, reserving the marinade in the bowl. Brown the meat on all sides to seal in the flavor.

5. Once the meat has browned, add the thyme and 2 cups of boiling water. Cover the pan and lower the heat to medium-low to simmer for about 1 hour.

6. Add the reserved marinade, diced onions, and 2 more cups of water; bring to a boil on high heat.

7. Add the tomato paste and simmer on low heat for another hour until the meat starts falling off of the bone. Adjust seasoning if necessary.

8. Serve with rice and hot sauce!

Curry goat being cooked outdoors in Jamaica.

VEAL MADEIRA

1 pound veal
scallopini – pounded
and flattened

2 tablespoons butter

1 cup mushrooms – sliced

2 shallots – minced

2 garlic cloves – minced

½ cup good quality
Madeira wine

½ cup chicken stock

⅓ cup heavy cream

1 tablespoon vegetable oil

Freshly ground black pepper

Flour, for dredging

Salt to taste

1. Season the veal on both sides with salt and pepper and lightly dredge in flour.

2. Pour the oil into a skillet over high heat and heat until hot but not smoking.

3. Add 1 tablespoon of butter to the pan, then sauté the veal, cooking for 1 minute on each side until golden brown and crispy. Transfer the veal to a warm plate and set aside.

4. Place the remaining butter in the pan and sauté the mushrooms and shallots until softened, about 3-5 minutes.

5. Add the garlic and sauté 30 seconds more.

6. Add the Madeira and scrape the bottom of the pan with a wooden spoon. When the wine has reduced by half, add the chicken stock and cook for 3 minutes or until the volume reduces by another half.

7. Add the heavy cream and cook for 3-4 minutes, until the sauce has thickened and coats the back of a spoon.

8. Season with salt and pepper to taste and return the veal to the skillet to heat through, about 1 ½ minutes.

9. Serve immediately with the sauce spooned over the veal.

I spent three days on the Portuguese island of Madeira. I toured the entire southern half of the island, drove through their famous natural "car wash" – a waterfall running off the face of the mountain and cascading right into the middle of the road, saw the natural lava pools in Porto Muniz, sailed on the sea and watched dolphins swim alongside the boat, and drove through the crazy number of tunnels that this tiny island has. Locals refer to Madeira as the Swiss cheese island because of the amount of holes that the tunnels create throughout it.

I went to Madeira Island to learn about Madeira wine because I love the flavor it gives to dishes. I have also felt like it's a dying cooking wine and wanted to get to it before it disappears.

I learned from local growers that Madeira has such an interesting and accidental evolution dating back to the Age of Exploration when Madeira was a standard port of call for ships heading to the Americas or India. On the long voyages, especially to India, the wines would be exposed to excessive heat which transformed the flavor of the wine. This was discovered by the wine producers of Madeira when an unsold shipment of wine returned to the islands after a round trip journey and it was consumed. The taste of Madeira wine was good enough for trade prior to this discovery and certainly provided the typical high that its consumers were looking for, but the exposure to heat made the wine a robust sweet wine that became popular for its use in cooking. Today, Madeira is noted for its unique wine-making process which involves heating the wine.

I ate Veal Madeira while in Lisbon and absolutely loved the flavors that the Madeira wine added. I had to learn how to make a Madeira dish in Madeira! I learned how to make Veal Madeira while there and realized it's much simpler than I expected. With very few ingredients and a fast cooking time, this is one of those impressive dishes that takes very little effort to make.

ASIAN SKIRT STEAK

2 pounds skirt steak – cleaned and trimmed

6 ounces hoisin sauce

6 ounces orange juice

3-4 dried red Thai chili peppers

1 tablespoon ginger – minced

1 tablespoon lemongrass pulp

1. In a large bowl, mix all ingredients together aside from the skirt steak.

2. Add the skirt steak to the marinade and place the bowl in the refrigerator; let the flavors marry for at least 4 hours. This recipe turns out best if the skirt steak is marinated overnight.

3. Once ready to grill, remove the skirt steak from the marinade. Heat a barbecue grill or a cast iron or grill pan on the stove on high heat.

4. Grill the steak for 3-4 minutes on each side on high heat for a medium steak. Skirt steak typically should not be cooked over medium doneness to avoid chewiness.

5. Remove the steak when done and let it rest for 10 minutes.

6. Slice the steak against the grain and serve.

For additional sauciness with your steak, pour some olive oil into a sauce pan and add the remaining marinade along with a half cup of beef stock; boil and add cornstarch to thicken. Drizzle on the steak and top with sliced scallions.

My favorite way to eat this Asian-flavored steak is with Pineapple Fried Rice (p. 225) or in tacos with a spicy slaw. Skirt steak is one of my favorite grilled meats because it does a great job of soaking in the marinade like a sponge. The quick cooking time makes this perfect for a summer barbecue party!

JUNGLEE MUTTON

2 pounds bone-in mutton (or goat meat)

10 garlic cloves – roughly chopped

15-20 dried red chilis

2 teaspoons coriander powder

2 tablespoons Kashmiri chili (optional)

½ cup ghee or clarified butter

Water as needed

Salt to taste

1. Cut the mutton into equally sized 1-inch pieces.

2. Heat the ghee in a cast iron pan on high heat, then add the meat.

3. Stir the meat for about 10-12 minutes until brown on all sides.

4. Add whole red chilis, salt, coriander, Kashmiri chili (if using), and garlic cloves.

5. Cover the pan and cook on low heat for 2 hours until the mutton becomes tender and the meat starts to come off the bone. If the meat starts to dry, add a few tablespoons of water. There should be enough water in the pan to keep the meat wet, but not so much that the meat boils.

I first had Junglee Mutton in Rajasthan, India, a colorful state in India with stunning royal palaces, historic forts, desert landscapes, and a rich cultural history full of kings and queens. Junglee is a hindi word that translates to "wild," and the dish was named as such because hundreds of years ago it was made with wild game that was caught in the jungles of Rajasthan. It was cooked with spices and butter because tomatoes and other vegetables were not available then. This fiery dish was loved by royalty and eaten with butter-laden roti (Indian flatbread).

Another common name for Junglee Mutton in Rajasthan is *Laal Maas* which translates to "red meat," a literal translation of the dish's appearance. I learned how to make this dish while I visited Rajasthan, after eating the dish at the hotel in which I was staying. It was spicy on its own, but when eaten with roti and yogurt, it was a perfectly-spicy and meaty dish. I was surprised to learn how minimal the ingredients were when used to make this dish loved by royalty years ago!

Serve hot Junglee Mutton with rice or bread. To cut down the spiciness, serve this dish alongside cool yogurt mixed with cucumber.

Aravali hills as seen from Nahargarh Fort in Jaipur, Rajasthan

SOUTH AFRICAN BEEF TRINCHADO

1 pound beef tenderloin – cubed

3 tablespoons butter

½ teaspoon salt

½ teaspoon black pepper

½ teaspoon paprika

2 ½ tablespoons Worcestershire sauce

2 small hot red chili peppers – stemmed and chopped (retain the seeds)

1 onion – sliced

4 garlic cloves – minced

1 tablespoon flour

½ cup beef stock

½ cup Portuguese red wine (Duoro Red)*

3-4 Portuguese bread rolls for dipping (or regular bread rolls)

Salt and pepper to taste

*If you cannot find a Duoro Red, a Cabernet Sauvignon can be substituted.

1. In a bowl, mix together the Worcestershire sauce, chilis, paprika, salt, and black pepper.

2. Add the cubed beef and let it marinate for 2 hours in the refrigerator to ensure that even the tougher cuts of meat are tender.

3. In a large saucepan on medium to high heat, heat 1 tablespoon of the butter.

4. When the butter is melted and sizzling, add about half of the beef and brown well.

5. Remove the beef cubes from the saucepan, place in a bowl and set aside.

6. Add 1 more tablespoon of butter to the saucepan and cook the remaining beef until browned. Set the meat aside in the same bowl.

7. Once done cooking the beef, reduce the heat to medium and add the final tablespoon of butter. Add the sliced onions and cook for about 5 minutes or until soft.

8. Add the garlic and cook for another minute or so. Sprinkle the flour over the onion/garlic mixture and stir for about 2 minutes or until thick.

9. Add the marinade, stock, and red wine to the pan until the sauce thickens, then simmer for about 10 minutes.

10. Add all of the cooked beef to the saucepan. Simmer for about 30 minutes on low heat or until the beef is tender and cooked. Season with salt and pepper to taste.

Camps Bay, Capetown, South Africa

In Capetown, I went paragliding off of Signal Hill. It was an exhilarating experience – running off a mountain, hoping that the parachute would inflate in time through enough momentum, while I was running against the wind. After what felt like a 20 second glide over Capetown, we landed on the beach in Camps Bay, an upscale beach locale. We headed over to Beach Road towards a string of bars and restaurants and settled into a spot with appropriate outdoor seating.

Savannah, a cider indigenous to South Africa, had become my daytime drink while I visited the country. I ordered a cider and took a look at the menu. Beef Trinchado was listed on the menu with the description, "Portuguese Peasant Beef Stew." The waitress explained that the dish originated from neighboring Mozambique during a time of Portuguese occupation and was influenced by their love of chili peppers.

Its flavors are perfect – meaty, saucy, and spicy, but not overpowered with chilis. Serve in bowls while hot, accompanied with fresh Portuguese bread rolls.

THAI BOAT NOODLES

6 garlic cloves – coarsely chopped

6 fresh coriander roots – cleaned and coarsely chopped

1 teaspoon whole black peppercorns

1 pound beef chuck steak or gravy steak – cut into 4-cm pieces

8 cups reduced salt chicken stock

2 lemongrass stems – bruised and cut into 4-cm strips

3 star anise pods

1 cinnamon stick

1 tablespoon dark soy sauce

¼ cup light soy sauce

2 cups dried rice vermicelli (or egg noodles)

2 cups bok choy – finely sliced

½ cup fresh Thai basil leaves

¼ cup fresh coriander – coarsely chopped

1 long fresh red chili – finely chopped

1 cup bean sprouts

1 tablespoon vegetable oil

Chili powder to taste

For the marinated pork

16 ounces pork fillet – thinly sliced

1 tablespoon light soy sauce

For the garlic oil

5 garlic cloves – coarsely chopped

¼ cup vegetable oil

1. Use a mortar and pestle to press the garlic, coriander, and peppercorns together to form a coarse paste.

2. Heat the oil in a large saucepan over high heat. Cook the beef for 2 minutes or until browned. Add the garlic mixture and cook for 1 minute. Add the stock, lemongrass, star anise, cinnamon, and soy sauces. Reduce the heat to low and gently simmer for 1 ½ hours.

3. Remove the beef with a slotted spoon, strain the broth to discard solids, and return the beef to the broth; set aside.

4. Meanwhile, combine the pork and soy sauce in a bowl; cover and place in the refrigerator to marinate.

5. To make the garlic oil, place the oil and garlic in a saucepan over medium heat. Cook for 2-3 minutes until the garlic just starts to turn golden brown. Pour the mixture into a heatproof bowl and set aside.

6. Boil a few cups of water in a large saucepan and cook the noodles for 2 minutes or until just tender. Drain and rinse them under cold water. Use scissors to cut the noodles into 6-inch pieces and divide amongst serving bowls.

7. Coarsely chop the beef into small pieces. Add the beef to the bowls along with the bok choy.

8. Return the stock to high heat until simmering. Place the marinated pork in the broth and simmer for 2 minutes or until just cooked. Divide the pork amongst the bowls.

9. Top each bowl with broth, basil, coriander, chili, and bean sprouts. Serve with garlic oil and chili powder.

"Suay" - Long Neck Village, Chiang Mai, Thailand

SEAFOOD

VADOUVAN SHRIMP

½ pound of small shrimp – peeled

2 eggs – beaten

6 tablespoons of Vadouvan seasoning*

6 tablespoons of cornmeal

Vegetable oil, for frying

To serve

Cilantro and yogurt mixture

Lime caviar (optional)

Vadouvan seasoning can be made at home by adding equal parts of dried shallots, onion powder, garlic powder, fennel seeds, turmeric powder, ground cardamom, ground cumin, mustard seeds, dried fenugreek leaves, ground thyme powder, cayenne pepper powder, black pepper, ground curry leaves, ground rosemary, ground nutmeg, and ground cloves. It is also readily available in South Asian markets.

1. Heat the vegetable oil in a saucepan (use enough vegetable oil so that it's ½-inch deep) or a deep fryer on medium heat.

2. Place the beaten eggs in a large bowl. Combine the cornmeal and Vadouvan seasoning in another large bowl.

3. Drop a handful of the shrimp into the beaten eggs and stir around so that each shrimp is coated.

4. Then take the shrimp from the beaten eggs and place into the seasoning bowl. Coat the shrimp with the flour and seasoning mixture.

5. Place the coated shrimp into the oil and fry until golden. Try not to stir the pot and don't place too many shrimp into the pot at once (make sure all the shrimp are touching the oil).

6. Using a slotted spoon, remove the shrimp and place on paper towels to absorb the excess oil. Repeat for the rest of the shrimp. Change the oil if there are too many solids in it.

7. Cool the shrimp for 10 minutes so that the outsides will get crisp. Enjoy on its own or serve with cilantro yogurt mixture and lime caviar.

The seaside promenade that runs along the Bay of Bengal in Pondicherry, India

Many people do not know that at one time the French owned a large part of the eastern coast of India known as the Coromandel Coast. Many have heard of the Dutch East Indian Company and British East Indian Company, but not many know that a French East Indian Company existed from the mid-1600s to the mid-20th century. It is during this time that the French took the local Madras curry powder under their wings.

They took the very strong, sharp curry powder made with the dominant flavors of curry leaves and fenugreek and toned it down with the addition of shallots, onions, and garlic. Shallots added a sweetness and calmness to the curry powder, garlic added another level of pungency but in a different direction than curry leaves, and onions came along for the ride just because the French felt like it. In other words, Vadouvan is the Frenchified version of a curry powder that the French developed to acclimate the dwellers of their French Empire to Indian flavors in East India.

When I came across this spice at the spice stall in London's Borough Market, the first thing that caught my attention was the name–Vadouvan. It just sounded like something that needed to be explored and so I did. I explored the story and I also explored how

I wanted to use it.

Just as the French would do, I paired this spice blend with a meat and finished it off with a generous amount of cream and butter. However, after I cooked it that way, I thought the actual flavors of the spice blend were hidden, even though it was tasty. Then I decided to use it liberally in seasoned flour to fry shrimp with and the rest of the components in this dish just came together.

The addition of lime caviar was something that came to me after having an unforgettable birthday meal on the French side of St. Martin. As I took a bite of a perfectly seared tuna, tiny bursts of sour drops exploded in my mouth almost like pop rocks! That night I learned all about lime caviar and added it to this dish.

REAL DEAL SAN FRANCISCO CRAB CAKES

10 pounds jumbo lump crab meat

2 ½ cups saltines – finely crushed

10 eggs

4 ½ cups mayonnaise

½ cup Dijon mustard

¼ cup Worcestershire sauce

¼ cup hot sauce

4 lemons – juice and zest

5 tablespoons Old Bay

¼ cup parsley – chopped

¼ cup tarragon – chopped

¼ cup chives – minced

For the tartar sauce

4 cups mayonnaise

¼ cup dill – finely chopped

⅛ cup capers – finely chopped

¼ cup cornichons – finely chopped

½ cup red onion – finely minced

⅛ cup tarragon – finely chopped

¼ cup parsley – finely chopped

¼ cup chives – finely minced

Juice of one lemon

1. Preheat oven to 350 degrees. Pick through crab meat to make sure there are no shells.

2. Mix together all ingredients for the crab cakes except for the crab meat and saltines. Using a rubber spatula, gently fold in the crab meat, trying not to break up the lumps.

3. Once the crab meat is mixed with the mayonnaise base, sprinkle in saltines and fold together. Allow the mixture to rest in a refrigerator for about 1 hour, until cold.

4. Using a 2-ounce ice cream scoop, scoop out crab cakes onto a parchment-lined sheet tray.

5. Place crab cakes in the oven and cook until golden brown on the outside but just warmed in the middle, about 10 minutes.

6. Meanwhile, make the tartar sauce. Using a mixing bowl and rubber spatula, mix all tartar sauce ingredients together and set aside. The sauce can be made a day ahead of the crab cakes.

7. Prepare a breading station by placing all-purpose flour in one bowl, whisked whole eggs in the second bowl and panko breadcrumbs in the third bowl.

8. Bread each crab cake by first dredging in the flour, followed by the egg wash, and finally by the panko breadcrumbs. Fry the crab cakes at 350 degrees until golden brown but just warmed in the middle, about 3 minutes.

My ideal afternoon in San Francisco includes riding a bicycle over the Golden Gate Bridge to Sausalito, then catching the Ferry back to Fisherman's Wharf, taking in the views of Alcatraz along the way, and finally walking along the wharf to have some of the best crab cakes I've ever had from the seaside shacks.

I've been making crab cakes since I graduated from college and became a professional. I started making them because they were easy to make yet an extremely elegant dish. I've made multiple versions with different types of spices, but nothing beats the original recipe especially when you have jumbo lump crab meat!

Golden Gate Bridge, San Francisco, California

CRAB RANGOON DIP

12 ounces cream cheese – softened to room temperature

1 cup sour cream

¾ cup shredded Monterey Jack

2 teaspoons soy sauce

1 tablespoon Sriracha (or any other hot sauce)

2 teaspoons garlic powder

8 ounces lump crab

1 cup green onions – sliced

Pita chips or wonton crisps, for serving

1. Preheat oven to 350 degrees.

2. In a large bowl, combine cream cheese, sour cream, Monterey Jack, soy sauce, Sriracha, and garlic powder. Mix together until evenly combined.

3. Add the crab and green onions. Mix well.

4. Transfer to a small baking pan 12x12-inch and bake for 20-25 minutes, until the dip is bubbly and beginning to turn golden brown.

5. Garnish with more green onions and drizzle with Sriracha, if desired. Serve warm with pita chips or wonton crisps for dipping.

Crab Rangoon holds a special place in my heart because it is the dish that I ordered in college from Chinese American restaurants if I wanted to be a bit more elegant that evening! It is a creamy, cheesy, crab-filled wonton that you can order as an appetizer. This version takes out the labor of stuffing the wontons and allows you to make the filling for an entire crowd.

SALMON HORS D'OEUVRE

1 pound salmon

2 teaspoons
ginger – finely minced

3 garlic cloves – finely
minced

2 green chilis – finely minced

1 teaspoon cumin

1 teaspoon turmeric

1 egg

1 tablespoon breadcrumbs

1 cup cilantro – finely
chopped

1 avocado – cut into
thin slices

1 lime – cut into wedges

20 crackers

1 teaspoon salt

1 tablespoon olive oil

1. Place the salmon in a food processor and pulse until the salmon is ground.

2. In a large bowl, add the salmon and all of the remaining ingredients, except for the olive oil and avocado. Mix well.

3. Scoop ½ tablespoon of the mix and form it into tiny patties. Continue forming the patties until all of the fish is used.

4. In a frying pan on medium-high heat, add the olive oil. Fry each salmon patty for 3-4 minutes on each side. Once a slight crust forms on each side, remove the patties from the pan.

5. Place each patty on a cracker and top with a slice of avocado. Repeat until all crackers are used.

Garnish the serving platter with lime wedges and enjoy!

A typical masala dhaba or spice box similar to this is a staple pantry item in every Indian kitchen.

THAI STYLE TUNA FISH LETTUCE WRAPS

1 can of organic packed tuna

1 tablespoon ground
ginger powder

1 tablespoon dried
lemongrass powder or paste

1 tablespoon dried
garlic powder

1 tablespoon dried mint

1 tablespoon brown sugar

1 Thai red chili – chopped

1 teaspoon ground
black pepper

1 teaspoon ground
white pepper

¼ teaspoon ground cumin

¼ cup cilantro – chopped

1 tablespoon olive oil

Salt to taste

To assemble

1 package Boston
lettuce – removed from stem

1 cucumber – sliced
lengthwise

Green onions – chopped

Lime wedges

1. Mix all of the dry ingredients in a bowl and keep aside.

2. In a non-stick pan on low heat, add olive oil and red chili and stir
    for a minute.

3. Add tuna and all of the dry ingredients. Stir well for 5 minutes.

4. Add cilantro and stir, then add salt to taste.

5. To serve, scoop tuna into lettuce leaves, add a cucumber slice, and
    garnish with lime wedges and green onions. Roll up your lettuce
    wraps and take a bite out of Thailand!

When I visited Thailand, I found a multitude of flavors, with lemongrass, ginger, and cumin being the dominant flavors that stuck with me. While I expected to find flavors like these, there was another flavor I didn't quite expect. I did not expect to taste an abundance of seafood flavors, even in dishes that did not contain any visible seafood. It took me some time to get used to this flavor surprise, because I was expecting sweet and spicy cuisine, like I had in Malaysia. Somewhere during my two week trip gallivanting around Thailand, I fell in love with the use of fish sauce, seafood broth, and all things seafood in Thai cuisine!

Growing up, tuna fish was my second favorite sandwich after ham and cheese and still to this day, I enjoy making tuna salad sandwiches for lunch. One day, I had an "Aha!" moment when I thought to actually cook the tuna with a curry-type seasoning and skip the typical cold mayonnaise, shallot, and hot sauce mixture. I went with some of the Thai flavors I was inspired by during my trip and just love this new spin on a tuna fish sandwich!

PRETZEL CRUSTED CALAMARI

**1 pound calamari – cut
into thick rings**

4 egg whites – beaten

**1 ½ cups unsalted
pretzels – ground
into a powder**

½ cup flour

**2 cups vegetable
oil, for frying**

Freshly ground pepper

Salt to taste

1. In a large bowl, beat the egg whites, then mix in the calamari. Let the calamari sit in the egg whites for 2 minutes.

2. In another large bowl, mix together the flour and unsalted pretzel powder.

3. Drop the calamari into the flour mixture and mix until each calamari ring is coated.

4. Heat the oil in a deep, heavy pan until the oil is around 350 degrees, and a sprinkle of the flour mixture sizzles when dropped in the pan.

5. Fry the calamari in batches until brown and crispy, about 4-5 minutes.

6. Remove the calamari and place on a paper towel-lined plate.

7. Sprinkle with salt and pepper and serve.

I love serving these with my Piccalilli Sauce (p. 8) for a play on pretzels with mustard!

Pretzel Crusted Calamari
with Piccalilli sauce

MIDYE DOLMASI–TURKISH STUFFED MUSSELS

For a party, I would triple this recipe and serve them in a large tin bucket.

30 large black mussels–cleaned and bearded

2 tablespoons dried currants (or cranberries)

2 tablespoons pine nuts

2 large onions–finely chopped

3 garlic cloves–minced

½ cup short-grain rice

1 tomato–very finely chopped or grated

⅓ cup flat leaf parsley–finely chopped

⅓ cup fresh dill–finely chopped

1 tablespoon tomato paste

2 teaspoons ground black pepper

½ teaspoon red pepper flakes (or chili flakes)

1 teaspoon ground cinnamon

¼ teaspoon nutmeg

1 cup hot water

4 tablespoons olive oil

Lemon wedges to serve

Salt to taste

1. Soak the mussels in warm water until they begin to open slightly.

2. Working quickly, insert the point of a knife into the opening, cutting the muscle that attaches the mussel to the shell. Gently pry open the shell a bit; do not break the hinge. (It's a learned maneuver, so don't be discouraged if the first few don't go so well.) Repeat with all the mussels, then rinse and refrigerate.

3. Soak the currants/cranberries in warm water for about 15 minutes, then drain.

4. Meanwhile, add the rice to a large bowl and rinse the rice.

5. Bring 2 cups of water to a boil and then keep on a simmer until used.

6. In a saucepan, heat the oil on medium heat and add the pine nuts, onions, garlic, nutmeg, and cinnamon. Stir until the pine nuts begin to brown and the onions are translucent.

7. Stir in the drained rice, tomato, tomato paste, red pepper flakes, black pepper, and drained currants/cranberries, and cook about 4 minutes.

8. Add the salt and just enough of the simmering water to cover the rice completely.

9. Lower the heat and cover the rice, cooking about 15 minutes, or until the liquid has absorbed.

10. Add half of the dill and all of the parsley, using a fork to break the rice apart and incorporate the herbs.

11. Set the rice aside and let it cool.

12. To finish, use a steamer rack or colander that fits into a large pot with a lid. Add enough water to the pot so that it comes nearly to the rack or colander bottom.

13. Spoon a generous amount of the rice mixture into each mussel. Pressing it closed as much as possible, clean off the outside of the shell. Stack each mussel into the prepared pot and cover them with a piece of parchment to allow for multiple stacks. (I have also used mini rubber bands to hold each mussel together.)

14. Weigh the mussels down, keeping them as closed as possible with a plate. Cover the pot and bring the water to a boil. Then lower the heat to a simmer and cook about 12 minutes.

15. Remove the pot from the heat and let the mussels cool covered in the pot for at least 1 hour before serving. They may also be refrigerated once they come to room temperature and served chilled.

16. To serve, stack the mussels on a platter and top with the remaining dill. Serve lemon wedges on the side to squeeze onto each mussel just like it is eaten on the streets and beaches of Turkey!

Midye Dolmasi, aromatic rice-stuffed mussels filled with herbs and spices, is a delicious street and beach-side snack that the Turkish love. In Istanbul, mostly in the Beyoglu District which is on the European side, carts are set up in the afternoon and stay open until all of the mussels sell out. Standing at a street cart, I've eaten 20 of these mussels in one go, but apparently that's nothing compared to the locals!

The ingredients do not vary much from one street cart to the next, making the authentic recipe quite easy to replicate in your own home. The difficult part of this recipe is stuffing the mussels with the rice and recreating the typical surprise. When ordering these at a street cart, it seems as though the mussels are uncooked since they appear closed, but once you order, the vendor cracks open each shell to reveal an already cooked mussel stuffed with aromatic rice—a trick for the eyes and my favorite memory of eating these! This recipe comes from a street vendor who told me all about it while I was eating them.

Authentic Midya Dolmasi served streetside in the Istiklal province of Istanbul, Turkey

AMRITSARI STYLE NEETA'S FISH FRY

1 pound boneless white-flesh fish (such as cod, flounder, or haddock)

2 teaspoons Kashmiri chili powder

½ teaspoon turmeric powder

1 teaspoon ginger – minced

2 garlic cloves – minced

1 green chili – finely chopped

½ teaspoon carom seeds

3 tablespoons gram flour

2 tablespoons cornflour

1 tablespoon white vinegar (or lemon juice)

1 teaspoon salt

Vegetable oil, for deep frying

Indian chaat masala (optional)*

*This spice blend can be found in South Asian grocery stores.

1. In a large bowl, add all of the ingredients except the fish and the oil. Mix well.

2. Carefully mix the fish into the batter to ensure all of the fish pieces are coated in the batter.

3. Heat the oil in a pan for deep frying. Carefully drop in the fish pieces one by one and fry until their crust is golden red and crisp.

4. Remove the fish with a slotted spoon and place them on a paper towel-lined plate to drain the oil.

5. Sprinkle with store-bought chaat masala, if using, and serve!

I was staying in the state of Punjab, India with relatives who are vegetarian and don't even like speaking about any type of meat. On the contrary, I am admittedly a meat lover and eat something meat-related almost every day. I was there doing research on a certain type of oil and the group I was there with was staying at a nearby hotel, enjoying daily doses of carnivorous gluttony. I was jealous – seriously jealous.

So one day, I did my research on the best non-vegetarian food in the area and snuck out for lunch with the crew. We went straight to a restaurant called Neeta's in a city called Phagwara whose specialty is a fried fish that is actually really popular in another city called Amritsar. Every Indian restaurant in the world has their own version of this fish using different types of flour, chili, or oil. However, the ingredients in this recipe that I've shared are used to make a traditional Amritsari fish.

Amritsari fish in Amritsar, India

Amritsari fish being fried in Amritsar, India

CARIBBEAN CONCH FRITTERS

¾ cup all-purpose flour

1 egg

½ cup milk

1 cup chopped conch meat (substitute lobster if conch is unavailable)

½ medium white onion – chopped

½ green pepper – chopped

2 celery stalks – finely minced

2 garlic cloves – finely minced

Salt and pepper to taste

Vegetable oil, for frying

Tabasco sauce to taste

1. In a large pot or deep fryer, heat oil to 365 degrees.

2. While the oil is heating, mix the flour, egg, and milk in a large bowl. Season with salt, pepper, and Tabasco sauce.

3. Mix in the chopped conch meat, onion, green pepper, celery, and garlic until well-blended.

4. Drop rounded tablespoons of the mixture into the hot oil and fry until golden brown; drain on paper towels.

5. Serve with ketchup, mayonnaise, or your choice of dipping sauce on the side.

These fritters are a must-have when I visit any Caribbean island. There are subtle differences from island to island, but all in all, they are dependably similar. This recipe is a crispy, fried taste of the ocean, which you can now make at home!

Live conch underwater

GAMBAS AL AJILLO

2 tablespoons butter

1 pound medium-sized shrimp – peeled and deveined

4 garlic cloves – finely sliced

2 tablespoons lemon juice

2 tablespoons dry sherry

2 teaspoons mustard

½ teaspoon paprika

1 dried red chili pepper – crushed

1 tablespoon parsley – minced

4 tablespoons olive oil

Freshly ground pepper to taste

Salt to taste

1. Heat the oil and butter in a frying pan.

2. Add the shrimp and garlic and sauté over high heat for 2-3 minutes.

3. Add the lemon juice, sherry, mustard, paprika, chili pepper, salt, and pepper. Mix well for a minute.

4. Sprinkle with parsley and serve.

This is a perfect dish to have with crusty bread for dipping. I ate this almost every day that I was in Portugal. The mustard is a special ingredient that I've only tasted in the Portuguese version of Gambas al Ajillo.

Arroz Puttanesca

1 cup short-grain rice

3 tablespoons capers

1 cup black olive rings

2 cups tomatoes – chopped

1 quart fish broth

1 tablespoon
anchovies – minced

½ cup basil leaves

4 garlic cloves – chopped

1 tablespoon olive oil

Mixed seafood*

Salt to taste

*Your preference of uncooked seafood.
I use shrimp, mussels, octopus, clams,
and squid.

1. In a large pot, add olive oil, garlic and anchovies; sauté until the garlic is slightly brown.

2. Add tomatoes and sauté until the tomatoes turn into a lumpy sauce and separate from the oil.

3. Add rice, fish broth, capers, and olives. Cook until the rice is almost al dente – approximately 15 minutes.

4. Add seafood and basil, stir, and cook until the seafood has cooked through – amount of time depends on the type of seafood.

5. Add salt to taste and stir.

This meal was inspired by a seafood and rice dish that I ordered in Mallorca, Spain. I added an Italian twist by using puttanesca flavors – olives, capers, and anchovies. Ladle the rice into bowls and serve with a lemon wedge.

A restaurant in Palma, Mallorca

Korean Chilean Sea Bass

1 pound Chilean sea bass

2 tablespoons Gochujang paste*

1 teaspoon rice wine vinegar

1 tablespoon soy sauce

1 tablespoon honey

This is a Korean red bean paste that is slightly spicy and can be found in most major grocery stores and Asian food markets.

1. Mix all of the wet ingredients and adjust seasoning based on your preference, i.e., more honey for sweet, more Gochujang for spice, more soy sauce for salt, or more rice wine vinegar for acid.

2. Cut the sea bass into desired portions.

3. Place the sea bass in a shallow bowl and pour the marinade over the fish. Mix with a wooden spoon to ensure each fillet is evenly coated.

4. Let the fish marinate for 15-20 minutes in the refrigerator.

5. Turn oven on broil and ensure the oven rack is on the second grate closest to the flame.

6. Cover an oven-proof tray with foil and place the marinated fish on the tray.

7. Cook fish on broil until the top has a slightly brown char, about 10-15 minutes.

8. Remove and serve with sautéed bok choy.

Gochujang is a thick, savory, funky, beautiful dark red fermented chili paste that has become quite popular amongst food lovers over the past few years. The sauce has been a staple ingredient in Korean households for hundreds of years and has been dominantly used in stews or as a chili sauce in the iconic Korean dish, Bibimbap.

I came across the sauce while exploring K-town in New York City and noted Gochujang while discussing Bibimbap's ingredients with a local restaurant owner. I purchased a bottle from a nearby Asian grocery store, brought it home and experimented with it. This recipe just came together while I was mixing a bunch of different sauces that I thought might create an umami flavor.

Chilean sea bass is by far my favorite type of fish because of its naturally buttery flavor and elegance. My new sauce paired perfectly with sea bass, and it's still a crowd favorite every time I make it!

SINGAPOREAN CRAB

1 pound mud crabs
or soft-shell crabs

4 tablespoons plain flour
(if using soft-shell crabs)

8 garlic cloves – roughly
chopped

8 fresh red chilis – roughly
chopped

1 egg

2 scallions – cut into
finger length pieces

1 teaspoon freshly-
squeezed lime

1 small bunch
cilantro – chopped

1 tablespoon vegetable oil

Vegetable oil, for frying
(if using soft-shell crabs)

Mix together for sauce

1 cup of water

5 tablespoons ketchup

1 ½ to 3 tablespoons
sugar, adjust to taste

1 ½ teaspoons cornflour

1 teaspoon dark soy
sauce or dark miso

¼ teaspoon salt

1. Heat the oil in a wok or shallow saucepan over high heat.

2. Add garlic and stir-fry for 1 minute.

3. Add the chilis and stir-fry until fragrant. For mud crabs, add them at this stage. Fry well until the shells start turning red. Then add the sauce ingredients, stir well, cover with lid, and simmer until the shells are completely red.

4. Break the eggs into the wok and streak with a fork; simmer until cooked. Squeeze lime juice over the eggs and stir in scallions and cilantro.

5. For soft-shell crabs, cut each crab into four, dry well, dredge in flour and deep fry until golden brown and crispy. Make the sauce as above, but omit the mud crabs. Toss soft-shell crabs in sauce just before serving.

It's well-known amongst native Singaporeans that this classic dish, served all over the country in both restaurants and hawker markets, began in the 1950s with a husband and wife.

When I had this dish at a market in Singapore, I asked the stall owner how its popularity began. He said it started with a man getting bored of his wife's daily steamed crab recipe and asking her to give it some pizazz. She came back with a version that had tomatoes, sugar, and soy sauce. Her husband approved and so she went on to serve it to family and friends who then urged her to open a street-side stall.

She did and it became wildly popular. While her original dish was on the sweeter side, over the years, many changes were made. Street stall vendors and restaurant owners added more chilis and what has now become the signature egg added just before serving.

Chili Crab at Telok Ayer Hawker Market - a food court loved by locals

GOAN MUSSELS

2 pounds fresh mussels
in the shell – scrubbed
and rinsed

¼ cup coriander seeds

1 ½ tablespoons cumin seeds

1 tablespoon whole
black peppercorns

5 ½ ounces white vinegar

2 ounces shredded
unsweetened coconut

1 inch knob of
ginger – finely chopped

5 garlic cloves – finely
chopped

1 large green
chili – finely chopped

1 white onion – chopped

1 medium ripe
tomato – diced

10 fresh curry leaves

½ ounce fresh
turmeric – peeled
and finely grated

1 tablespoon red
chili powder

8 ounces unsweetened
coconut milk

1 cup cooked ramen noodles

1 tablespoon olive oil

Sea salt to taste

1. Heat a medium sauté pan over medium heat.

2. Add the coriander seeds, cumin seeds, and peppercorns. Stir constantly until the seeds become toasted and fragrant, 3-4 minutes. Cool completely.

3. To make the paste, grind the coriander seeds, cumin seeds, peppercorns, and a pinch of salt using a mortar and pestle or a spice grinder.

4. Transfer the spice mixture to a food processor. Add the vinegar, coconut, ginger, garlic, chili, and onions; blend to form a paste.

5. Heat the oil in a heavy, large, wide pot over low heat. Add the paste and sauté until fragrant and some of the juices have evaporated, 5-10 minutes.

6. Add the tomato, curry leaves, turmeric, chili powder, and a pinch of salt. Stir and cook until the tomato pieces are tender and melting into the sauce, 5 minutes.

7. Add the mussels and 4 ½ ounces of water, increase the heat to medium and cover the pot for about 4-5 minutes.

8. Uncover and check to see that most of the mussels have opened. Discard any mussels that have not opened after 6 minutes.

9. Reduce the heat to low, then mix in the coconut milk and simmer for 2-3 minutes to allow the flavors to blend.

To serve, divide the mussels among bowls with ramen on the bottom and a lemon wedge on the side.

Thai Shrimp Po'boy

For the Thai curry paste*

½ teaspoon coriander seeds
(or ground coriander)

1 teaspoon cumin seeds (or ground cumin)

½ teaspoon black peppercorns (or ½
teaspoon ground black pepper)

1 red bell pepper – seeds
removed and chopped

2-4 Thai red chilis (or substitute
with another hot red chili pepper)

1 lemongrass stalk – root and
tip trimmed, then chopped

2 teaspoons ground ginger or
galangal powder (or 1 tablespoon
fresh ginger/galangal)

3 garlic cloves – skins removed

1 teaspoon ground turmeric

3 tablespoons lemon juice

1 lime – zested and juiced

½ cup diced shallots

1 tablespoon honey or maple syrup

½ teaspoon sea salt, plus more to taste

2-3 tablespoons olive oil

Ingredients

2 pounds medium-sized (41/50 count)
shrimp – peeled and deveined

2 tablespoons Thai curry paste

1 cup coconut milk

1 ½ cups all-purpose flour

1 cup cornmeal

4 (8-inch long) French
rolls – split horizontally

1 cup iceberg lettuce – shredded

½ cup sliced tomatoes

Hot sauce to taste

Vegetable oil, for frying

To minimize time, store-bought Thai curry paste can be used as well.

1. To make the curry paste, place the first 15 ingredients in a food processor and blend until a paste is formed. To store the paste, place in an airtight jar or container in the refrigerator for up to 1 ½ weeks.

2. To make the shrimp, whisk together 2 tablespoons of curry paste with coconut milk in a large bowl. Add the shrimp and mix well, then let the shrimp marinate in the refrigerator for 1 hour.

3. In another bowl, mix together the flour and cornmeal.

4. Place a frying pan on medium-high heat and add the vegetable oil for deep frying.

5. Once the oil is hot enough, remove the shrimp from the marinade one by one, coat in the flour mixture, and fry the shrimp until golden brown while stirring occasionally, about 4 minutes per batch. Remove the shrimp with a slotted spoon and transfer to a paper towel to drain.

6. Open the rolls and spread the faces with mayonnaise; top with lettuce, tomato, and shrimp. Serve with hot sauce, if desired.

The Po'boy is an iconic sandwich in New Orleans, Louisiana, one that is even better known than the Muffuletta. There is a wide variety of Po'boy fillings served throughout New Orleans including one filled with fried soft-shell crab. Despite the variety, one ingredient remained the same across all of the Po'boys that I tried in New Orleans–a crusty, hollowed-out French baguette. The bread serves as a vehicle to hold crispy, fried shrimp along with loads of fixins and a remoulade sauce.

I wanted to introduce a twist in this classic recipe by flavoring the sandwich with Thai seasonings. Admittedly, it's not a sandwich I make often, but when I do, I thoroughly enjoy every single bite!

JAMAICAN ESCOVITCH FISH

1 pound cod or haddock
fillet – cut into large cubes

1 onion – sliced

¼ cup carrots – sliced

¼ cup mixed peppers – sliced

1 bunch spring
onions – roughly chopped

1 teaspoon Scotch bonnet
peppers – sliced

½ teaspoon Jamaican
pimento seeds

2 cups flour

2 eggs – beaten

¼ cup milk

2 tablespoons black pepper,
plus an extra pinch

2 tablespoons paprika

½ cup white vinegar

1 cup vegetable oil

Salt to taste

1. To make the Escovitch dressing, put a frying pan on high heat and add 1 tablespoon of oil.

2. Add the sliced onion, ¼ cup of sliced carrots, ¼ cup of mixed peppers, spring onions, Scotch bonnet peppers, and pimento seeds to frying pan.

3. Add a pinch of black pepper and mix together.

4. Add the vinegar, mix well, and simmer for 10 minutes. Adjust seasoning for salt, remove from the heat and allow the mixture to completely cool down.

5. Season the fish with salt, 1 tablespoon paprika, and 1 tablespoon black pepper.

6. On a plate, mix together 1 tablespoon paprika, 1 tablespoon black pepper, flour and a pinch of salt.

7. In a bowl, whisk together the eggs and milk pour onto the fish fillets and let it sit for 5 minutes.

8. Place a frying pan on high heat and add 1 cup of vegetable oil. (When a vegetable piece sizzles in the pan the oil is ready for frying.)

9. Cover the fish in flour, then shake off any excess flour.

10. Fry the fish in the pan for 10 minutes on each side, until golden brown. Repeat until all fish fillets are fried.

11. Pour the Escovitch dressing on the fish and serve immediately.

This lightly fried fish dish is very typical in Jamaica and is usually made with Red Snapper. I used a different white-flesh fish that may be easier to find, because to me, what sets this dish apart and makes it Jamaican is the dressing which includes Jamaican pimento seeds, Scotch bonnet peppers, and mixed peppers.

Fishing boats on a
Jamaican beach

MADEIRA STYLE FISH WITH BANANAS

2 (8-ounce) fillets of black scabbard fish (or substitute with mackerel)

2 bananas

¼ teaspoon fresh oregano – chopped

¼ teaspoon fresh marjoram – chopped

1 garlic clove – minced

2 tablespoons flour

2 eggs (one for fish, one for bananas)

Breadcrumbs

Freshly ground black pepper to taste

Pinch of salt

Vegetable Oil, for frying

For the pineapple sauce

4 tablespoons mayonnaise

6 tablespoons pineapple juice

1 drop Tabasco

¼ cup orange juice

1. Rub the fish well with garlic and season with herbs, salt, and pepper.

2. Whisk one egg in a bowl and then pour into a flat plate. Pour the flour into a separate plate.

3. Dip the fish into the flour and then into the egg.

4. Heat oil in a wok on medium heat and fry the fish for 2-3 minutes, until golden yellow.

5. Whisk the second egg in bowl and then pour into a flat plate. Pour breadcrumbs into a separate plate.

6. Peel and halve the bananas; dip into whipped egg and then into the breadcrumbs. Fry in the heated oil until golden yellow.

7. For the sauce, mix together the mayonnaise, Tabasco and orange juice. Add the pineapple juice and serve cold with the fish.

Banana trees with unripe bananas and banana flowers in Madeira, Portugal

In Madeira, this is referred to as Scabbard and Banana. It's an odd combination and actually none of the elements of this dish on their own would qualify as a typical dish from Madeira. Unless of course you are buying them as locally-grown ingredients - the Scabbard fish which is found in the waters surrounding Madeira or their popular tiny bananas grown on the island. This dish in its totality is completely Madeiran and commonly eaten by locals.

CHERMOULA SARDINES

1 cup cilantro – finely chopped

4 garlic cloves – finely chopped

2 tablespoons cumin

2 tablespoons paprika

½ teaspoon cayenne pepper

¼ teaspoon saffron threads – crumbled

2 tablespoons lemon juice

1 teaspoon salt, plus more to taste

3 tablespoons vegetable oil

2 cups chickpea flour

5 pounds whole sardines – skin on and filleted

Vegetable oil, for frying

1. To make the chermoula sauce, blend the first 9 ingredients in a food processor until well-mixed.

2. Wash the sardines, place in a deep dish, and pour the chermoula sauce on the sardines. Mix well to make sure each piece is well-coated.

3. Place the chickpea flour in a shallow dish. Note that there is no need to season the chickpea flour as the chermoula coating on the fish provides enough seasoning.

4. Place enough vegetable oil in a frying pan for deep frying on medium to high heat.

5. When the oil is warm enough, coat each piece of the sardines in the flour and fry until golden brown, about 5-8 minutes total.

Chermoula is a Moroccan spice blend that is used in various dishes, but most commonly it's used to flavor fish. Even though I'm not a huge fan of sardines, this recipe worked wonders on my palate. The saltiness and oiliness of the sardines goes surprisingly well with the hint of sweetness and distinct flavor that the saffron gives to the chermoula. It's a perfect combination!

Variations of this recipe may include different types of flour, but a key component of this dish that makes it Moroccan is the use of chickpea flour which is widely used across Morocco to make tarts and flatbreads.

A sardine being prepared to fry with chermoula and farine "chickpea flour" in Morocco

INDIAN SPICED CEVICHE

**For Sher Ka Dood
(Lion's Milk)**

¼ inch fresh knob of
ginger – cut in half

1 garlic clove

½ cup cilantro
sprigs – roughly chopped

8 limes – juiced

1 green chili

1 teaspoon cumin powder

1 teaspoon coriander
powder

1 teaspoon pomegranate
powder

1 teaspoon red chili powder

½ teaspoon sea salt

For the ceviche

1 pound fresh sea bass
fillet (or other white
fish) – skinned and filleted

1 large red onion – diced

1 avocado – diced

1 cup pineapple – diced

1 red hot chili pepper – diced

1 teaspoon sea salt

A few cilantro sprigs – leaves
finely chopped

1. To make the Sher Ka Dood, blend all of the ingredients in a blender and transfer to a bowl. This can be kept in the refrigerator for up to 4 hours prior to making the ceviche.

2. To make the ceviche, rinse the onion and then leave it to soak in iced water for 10 minutes. Drain thoroughly, spread out on a paper towel or a clean kitchen towel to remove any excess water, and then place in the refrigerator until needed. This will reduce the strength of the onion and help to keep the slices crisp.

3. Cut the fish into uniform strips of around 1 ¼ by ¾ inch (3x2 cm). Place in a large bowl, add a pinch of salt, and mix together gently with a metal spoon. The salt will help open the fish's pores.

4. Leave the fish for 2 minutes and then pour over the Lion's Milk and combine gently with the spoon. Leave the fish to "cook" in this marinade for 10-15 minutes in the refrigerator.

5. When the fish turns opaque, it is done cooking.

6. Add the onion, cilantro, avocado, pineapple, and red peppers to the fish. Mix together gently with the spoon and taste to check that the balance of salt, sour, and chili is to your liking.

7. Divide among serving bowls and serve immediately with plantain or banana chips.

I call the spice mixture Sher Ka Dood because to take a sip of it solo takes the courage of a lion. This is a ceviche that I've made for multiple dinner parties and it never fails to impress!

BAJA FISH TACOS

For the cabbage slaw

5 cups (or one 10-ounce bag) shredded red cabbage

3 tablespoons red onion – minced

½ cup fresh cilantro – chopped

3 tablespoons apple cider vinegar

1 ½ teaspoons vegetable oil

Salt to taste

For the chipotle sauce

¾ cup mayonnaise

2 tablespoons lime juice

2-3 chipotle chilis in adobo sauce (canned) – roughly chopped

1 tablespoon honey

1 large garlic clove

For the beer batter

1 cup all-purpose flour

½ teaspoon ground black pepper

1 cup beer (Corona or similar)

1 teaspoon salt

For the fish and tortillas

1 ½ pounds skinless cod – cut into 1-inch wide by 4-inch long strips

12 (6-inch) soft corn tortillas – warmed

Lime wedges, for serving

Vegetable oil, for frying

1. Toss the cabbage, red onion, cilantro, vinegar, oil, and salt together in a medium bowl and refrigerate until ready for use.

2. Combine the mayonnaise, lime juice, chipotle with sauce, honey, and garlic in a blender or food processor and blend until smooth; refrigerate until ready for use.

3. Mix the flour, salt, and pepper together in a medium bowl. Slowly add the beer and whisk until the batter is smooth with no lumps and set aside.

4. In a deep frying pan on medium heat, add enough oil and heat the oil until a drop of the batter sizzles when dipped into the oil.

5. Working in batches, dip the fish strips in the beer batter and coat both sides.

6. Fry the fish until golden brown and cooked through, about 2 minutes per side. Transfer to a plate lined with paper towels to drain.

7. Smear each tortilla with a generous amount of the chipotle sauce, then top with the cabbage slaw. Place one piece of fish inside each tortilla and serve with lime wedges.

Fish tacos – a staple of Northwestern Mexico and Southern California. All of the components of this recipe are consistent across Baja-style fish tacos. All are typically beer battered and all have a cabbage slaw of sorts. My love of smoky chipotle peppers, which I cook with quite often, is what sets this recipe apart. The chipotle sauce pulls this recipe together and gives it a delicious makeover in my opinion!

MAINE LOBSTER ROLLS

2 pounds cooked lobster meat

½ cup mayonnaise

¼ celery–finely minced

4 hot dog buns–top split

2 tablespoons unsalted butter

¾ cup Boston lettuce–shredded

Few drops of Tabasco sauce

Juice of one lemon

1. Cut the lobster meat into ½-inch pieces, transfer to a strainer set over a bowl, and refrigerate for 1 hour. This will remove the water within the lobster.

2. In a large bowl, mix the lobster meat with the mayonnaise and season with salt and pepper.

3. Mix in the celery, lemon juice, and Tabasco sauce until well-blended. Add more or less Tabasco according to your desired level of heat.

4. Heat a large skillet, brush the sides of the hot dog buns with melted butter, and toast butter-side down over moderate heat until golden brown. Flip and repeat.

5. Transfer the hot dog buns to plates, fill them with the shredded lettuce and an overflowing portion of the lobster salad. Serve immediately.

This is an easy recipe mimicking the lobster rolls that are typically served seaside all throughout Maine. Some places make variations with diced onions, bacon, or parsley, but I particularly like this version because there's more room for the lobster, overstuffed in the bun, to shine through. These go perfectly with a glass of Prosecco and Old Bay spice potato chips!

Lobster traps on board in Maine

Sri Lankan Deviled Butter Shrimp

2 pounds raw medium shrimp – shelled and deveined

2 tablespoons butter

1 large onion – finely chopped

2 garlic cloves – finely chopped

2 cups cherry tomatoes – halved

2 teaspoons paprika

½ teaspoon chili powder

1 teaspoon ground turmeric

½ cup water

1 tablespoon tomato paste

1 tablespoon honey

2 teaspoons salt

1 tablespoon oil

1. Heat a frying pan on medium-high heat; add 1 tablespoon of oil and 2 tablespoons of the butter.

2. Add the onions and fry for a couple of minutes, then add the garlic. When the onions are translucent, add the cherry tomatoes and fry until they start to soften.

3. Add the paprika, salt, chili, and turmeric powder and fry for 1 minute. Add more butter if needed.

4. Add the prawns and fry for 3 minutes. Then add the water and tomato paste and stir for 5 minutes.

5. Add the honey, stir for a minute and serve immediately.

A delicacy in Sri Lanka and a sure shot crowd-pleaser!

MASALA GRILLED SHRIMP WITH CUCUMBER AND POMEGRANATE SALAD

For the shrimp

1 pound shrimp (about 10-12 count) – shelled and deveined

½ inch knob of ginger – chopped

2 garlic cloves – chopped

2 green chilis – chopped

1 tablespoon fresh lemon juice

2 teaspoons dried fenugreek leaves

1 tablespoon MDH Fish Masala*

1 teaspoon red chili powder

1 teaspoon sea salt

1 tablespoon olive oil

For the salad

Cucumber – diced

Pomegranate – peeled

Cilantro – chopped

Salt to taste

Tools

Bamboo skewers – soaked in water for 30 minutes

This spice blend can be found in South Asian grocery stores. If you cannot find it, omit from the recipe.

1. Mix all of the salad ingredients together and add salt according to taste. Keep refrigerated until you are ready to serve.

2. In a bowl big enough to hold the shrimp, add all of the shrimp ingredients and mix well so the shrimp are covered in the spice mixture.

3. Marinate in the refrigerator for 30-60 minutes.

4. Skewer shrimp on the bamboo skewers, then grill on medium/high heat for 2-3 minutes on each side, until the shrimp are cooked (pink in color).

Serve with mint chutney and a side salad, and enjoy!

BLOODY MARY CAJUN SHRIMP SALAD

1 pound shrimp – peeled and deveined (your desired size)

1 pound bacon (optional)

1 cup celery – finely diced

1 cup onions – finely diced

1 cup pepperoncini

1 cup pickled vegetables

1 tablespoon olive oil (optional)

For the Bloody Mary mix*

12 ounces tomato juice

4 teaspoons horseradish

2 teaspoons Worcestershire sauce

4 ounces vodka

Tabasco sauce to taste

Pinch of black pepper

Pinch of celery salt

For the Cajun spice blend mix*

2 teaspoons garlic powder

2 ½ teaspoons paprika

1 teaspoon black pepper

1 teaspoon onion powder

1 teaspoon cayenne pepper

1 teaspoon dried oregano

1 ¼ teaspoon dried thyme

1 teaspoon red pepper flakes

2 teaspoons salt

*To save time, you may buy your favorite Cajun spice blend and/or Bloody Mary mix.

1. Sprinkle the Cajun seasoning liberally onto the shrimp and mix well. Keep in the refrigerator until ready to cook.

2. If using bacon, fry the bacon in a frying pan until crisp, remove and crumble.

3. In the same pan, cook the shrimp in the bacon drippings or 1 tablespoon of olive oil.

4. When the shrimp turns pink, remove and keep on a plate.

5. Mix all of the Bloody Mary mix ingredients together and keep aside – adjust the seasonings to your liking.

6. In a large bowl, mix together the celery, onion, pepperoncini, pickled vegetables, and Bloody Mary mix.

7. Assemble the salad using martini glasses (or your preferred serving glass) by placing the salad at the bottom and topping with a few pieces of shrimp and crumbled bacon.

I've made this for dinner parties and guests are first drawn to the presentation, followed by the balance of soft and powerful flavors in one bite. The Cajun seasoning inspired by Louisiana, my favorite Bloody Mary recipe, and the optional bacon that I always add brings this dish together harmoniously!

"Mujer Fuerte" - Mural art in San Pancho, Mexico

VEGETARIAN

NEW ZEALAND CHEESE ROLL

1 loaf soft long white bread

2 cups cheddar cheese – grated

1 cup onions – finely chopped

1 cup evaporated milk

½ packet onion soup (or french onion dip powder)

Butter – melted

1. Preheat oven to 350 degrees.

2. In a saucepan on low heat, add the cheese, onions, evaporated milk, and onion soup or dip powder.

3. Keep stirring while allowing the ingredients to melt into a smooth mixture.

4. Once smooth, remove the mixture from heat and allow it to cool for a minute.

5. Spread a heaping spoon of the cheese on the bread and roll the bread into a log.

6. Place on a butter-greased baking tray and generously brush with butter.

7. Bake for 10-15 minutes until the bread turns golden brown.

8. Remove and serve immediately.

Homemade cheese rolls at a local home in Queenstown, New Zealand

My closest cousin moved from the UK to New Zealand, a country I was dying to see, and had also gotten engaged since I'd seen her last, so I had to go visit. I was excited to visit her and to see this breathtaking country. Cuisine-wise the only thing I had heard about were New Zealand's lamb chops and wine. I wasn't expecting to discover any spices or unveil any new trend that was going to be the next big "It" thing for foodies around the world. Admittedly, it was so judgmental of me! New Zealand is a country with many food traditions, culinary experimentation and unique crops that I was able to savor and talk about.

To give some background, my cousin and I had already traveled to several countries together before this trip. When I arrived to Auckland, she had only been living there with her fiancé for about 2 months. Everything was new to all of us as we explored together.

Since we knew about wine our first stop was a day trip to Waiheke Island, a hilly haven of beautiful vineyards and olive groves. We spent the entire day visiting wineries and had a lovely meal and a bottle of wine at the last vineyard we visited. Feeling giddy with joy, mostly because of the wine, but also because we were exploring New Zealand together, we took the ferry back to Auckland, laughing the entire way, and stumbled into the first watering hole that we saw– Botswana Butchery. The bar was situated on the water and with a buzz already started and a beautiful view, we continued to have glass after glass of wine. We were so excited to see each other, we discussed everything we were going to talk about during

Beautiful Milford Sound in Queenstown, New Zealand

the entire trip, went home, and invited gin to the party accompanied with dancing–we didn't sleep.

We had already planned an 8 a.m. flight to Queenstown for a few days. It was a painful morning and even more painful flight. I quickly passed out but woke up intermittently to get a glimpse of where we were. From what I saw, it looked like the most beautiful place on Earth. We desperately needed to snap out of our hangovers because we were in Queenstown for adventure and fun!

While waiting for baggage to arrive, I walked up to a juice and coffee kiosk and ordered a fresh orange juice. I also spotted a thick piece of bread rolled with something that looked like cheese. I asked the lovely man for the "New Zealand Cheese Roll" as noted on the sign next to it and he politely said it would take a few minutes to toast with butter on top. Butter? Yes please! He handed me a toasty, golden, glistening rolled bread and warned me that it was hot. I sipped my juice and waited about a minute, then took a bite.

Oh my–the flavored cheese and buttered crispy bread was exactly what I needed in that moment. I finished my juice and the cheese roll and was as good as new, ready to take on Queenstown! While I was just looking for a quick snack, I had no idea that what I just ate was considered a delicacy of the South Island, nicknamed *South Island sushi*. Only later did I find out that there were even cheese roll recipe contests and huge debates over the best version

Apparently even on days when I'm hungover and feel like staying in fetal position in bed all day, I manage to come across local cuisines! I've shared a very easy recipe that people in New Zealand follow for parties, sporting events, barbecues and shhhh... hangovers!

YOGURT KEBABS

2 cups Greek yogurt

2 green chilis – chopped

2 tablespoons
cilantro – chopped

1 small white
onion – finely chopped

1 teaspoon red chili powder

1 teaspoon roasted
cumin powder

1 teaspoon ground
cinnamon powder

¼ cup plain breadcrumbs

¼ cup cornflour, for
coating kebab patties

¼ cup roasted cashews
and peanuts – chopped

¼ cup raisins

1 lemon – cut into quarters

1 medium red
onion – thinly sliced

Salt to taste

Vegetable oil, for
shallow frying

1. Place the yogurt in a cheesecloth or a thin meshed strainer. Strain the water out for 1 hour by hanging the cloth on the kitchen faucet or placing the strainer over a bowl to catch the juices.

2. Add the strained yogurt to a medium-sized mixing bowl and add in green chilis, chopped cilantro, chopped white onions, red chili powder, roasted cumin powder, ground cinnamon, salt, and breadcrumbs. Mix well.

3. If the dough is sticky, you can add more breadcrumbs, but do not over-knead.

4. Scoop up a lemon-sized amount and roll it to make a ball.

5. If the dough sticks to your palms, then dampen or grease your hands.

6. Flatten the dough with your fingers and place a few nuts and raisins in the center.

7. Cover it by pressing the edges towards center to shape the dough into a kebab patty.

8. Prepare the other kebabs in the same way.

9. Pour the cornflour onto a flat plate and coat each kebab in the flour.

10. Heat oil in a pan and shallow fry the kebabs on medium heat until they turn golden brown.

11. Remove and place onto a paper towel.

12. Serve hot with sliced red onions, lemon wedges, and a dipping sauce of your choice!

This yogurt-based appetizer is fit for royalty! These kebabs have their roots in Awadhi cuisine which is native to Lucknow, India. Since the Awadh Empire was ruled by the Mughals from Persia, the cooking techniques and Persian palate heavily influenced the cuisine of that region.

The use of nuts, dried fruits, and yogurts, and the technique of pan frying the kebabs are what set the kebabs of this region apart from the traditional tandoor cooking method of the north. These days you can find these kebabs all over India and they are specifically popular at kebab houses in New Delhi. Bite into the crunchy exterior to find a spiced and creamy interior with just a touch of sweetness from the nuts and raisins.

CAMEMBERT DIP

1 large wheel Camembert cheese

2 garlic cloves – roasted

1 rosemary sprig

French bread, for dipping

1. Preheat oven to 350 degrees.

2. Take the cheese out of the wooden box and remove the cheese from the wrapper.

3. Cut a large cross through the top of the cheese and stick the roasted garlic pulp and rosemary leaves inside.

4. Place the cheese back in the box, put the lid on, and tie kitchen twine around the diameter of the box to keep it intact.

5. Put the box on a baking sheet in the center of the oven and bake for 15 minutes.

6. Remove from the oven, take off the lid, and peel back the rind to expose the runny center.

7. Place on a platter and serve with the bread.

This is such a simple and lush appetizer to prepare. Pair it with a bottle of wine and spend the rest of the night pretending you are gazing at the Eiffel Tower!

LIGURIAN FARINATA

4 cups water

2 ½ cups chickpea flour

1 tablespoon salt

¼ cup extra virgin olive oil

Freshly ground black pepper

Originated in Genoa and perfected over time.

1. Mix all of the ingredients except for the black pepper. Let the liquid mix rest for almost 4 hours at room temperature.

2. When ready to cook, preheat the oven to its highest temperature (usually 500-550 degrees). Ensure the baking rack is in the middle of the oven.

3. Spread the olive oil in an ovenproof baking dish or cast iron skillet. Make sure the entire pan is covered in olive oil.

4. Slowly start adding the mix into the baking dish and use a whisk to help maintain the texture. Sprinkle your desired amount of black pepper on top.

5. Switch the oven to broil and slide the baking dish/skillet into the oven.

6. Bake/broil until the top of the farinata shows a nice golden color and the mixture is set.

7. Remove from the oven and let the pancake cool before cutting into pie-shaped slices and serving.

You may also add rosemary when adding black pepper if you want extra flavor, however, this is the traditional recipe.

Farinata is one of the simplest yet most traditional Milanese dishes that a local took me to have in Genoa, the capital city of the crescent-shaped Liguria region of northwestern Italy. While there, I was told that it is considered peasant food because it is made with simple and inexpensive yet nutritious and filling ingredients.

Farinata has ancient origins. Greek and Roman soldiers used to prepare a sloppy mixture of chickpea flour and water, cooked in the hot sun on their metal shields, in order to fill up quickly and cheaply. Today, it is cooked in an extremely high heat pizza oven and then cut into large triangular slices.

My Milanese friend was so passionate when explaining this dish to me that his mouth was watering as he spoke! However, as he was explaining the ingredients and the process of making it, I didn't share the same excitement. It sounded too much like something I've had growing up–a Besan Chila or chickpea flour omelette.

Contrary to my hesitation and lack of excitement, Farinata has a very different taste and consistency than what I was comparing it to. It is crispy on the outside, soft on the inside, and subtly flavored with just salt and olive oil. There are still a few things that are necessary in order to make good Farinata–high temperature and good olive oil. If the oven is not hot enough, the results will be rubbery, uniform and completely lacking the crisp melt-in-your mouth consistency.

I told my Milanese friend that I fell in love with the flavors and simplicity of this Ligurian specialty after all and so he gave me his family recipe!

Pinky Out Patatas Bravas

1 pound small red
potatoes – sliced in half

2 tablespoons sage leaves

2 teaspoons truffle oil

1 tablespoon sliced truffles

2 tablespoons olive oil

Paprika

Sour cream

Sea salt

1. Pour olive oil into a flat frying pan on medium heat.

2. Add the potatoes and shallow fry until they are cooked within and crispy on the outer edges.

3. Add the sage leaves at the end, prior to removing potatoes from the skillet.

4. Plate the potatoes in a flat bowl, then sprinkle with sea salt and truffle oil.

5. Top the potatoes with sour cream, paprika, and sliced truffles.

My elegant twist on a well-known Spanish tapa. Use a toothpick to eat these with your pinky out!

Patatas Bravas in Spain

SIMPLE IRISH BOXTY RECIPE

1 cup raw potatoes – grated

1 cup leftover
mashed potatoes

1 cup all-purpose flour

2 teaspoons baking powder

2 eggs – beaten

¼ cup milk

1 cup clotted cream
(optional)

2 teaspoons salt

Butter or oil, for frying

The Giant's Causeway is an area of about 40,000 interlocking basalt columns, the result of an ancient volcanic eruption.

1. Place the grated raw potatoes in a clean cloth and twist to remove excess moisture.

2. Whisk together flour, salt, and baking powder.

3. Combine flour mixture with raw potatoes, mashed potatoes, milk and eggs.

4. Heat a heavy skillet over medium heat for shallow frying and add butter or oil.

5. Drop potato batter by the tablespoon into the hot pan.

6. Brown on both sides, about 4 minutes per side.

7. Butter each boxty and serve hot with clotted cream.

Boxty is a traditional Irish potato pancake – part pancake, part hash brown – native to Co Leitrim and the Northwest of Ireland. Its origin dates back to before the famine when it was so popular that it inspired folk rhymes: "Boxty on the griddle, Boxty on the pan, if you can't make Boxty, you'll never get a man!"

It's the perfect way to use leftover mashed potatoes!

Pan con Tomate

2 large tomatoes

1 loaf ciabatta – split
in half horizontally

2 medium garlic
cloves – split in half

Sea salt

Extra virgin olive oil

1. Split tomatoes in half horizontally and grate them into a large bowl using a box grater. Keep the skin intact while grating.

2. Once all of the flesh is grated, discard the skin and season the tomato pulp with kosher salt to taste.

3. Drizzle oil on the bread, cut-side face up and, season with the sea salt.

4. Toast the bread until crisp and rub with split garlic cloves as soon as it's removed from the oven.

5. Spoon the tomato mixture over the bread and drizzle with a little more olive oil and sea salt.

Serve immediately with some red wine or sangria!

Casa Batlló, one of Antoni Gaudí's masterpieces in Barcelona, Spain

Pan con tomate is one of the simplest, most loved, and widely eaten dishes from Cataluña. *Pa amb tomàquet* is probably the most representative dish of the Catalan cuisine, though it is also very popular in Valencia and Baleares, where it is known as *pa amb oli* (bread with oil).

I noticed this dish being consumed during all hours of the day while living in Valencia for a month, but when it caught my eye most was during my 8:45 a.m. walks rushing to yoga with coffee in my hand. I saw locals getting their morning coffee (cortado preferably) along with bread that was slathered in a little bit of red sauce. For about a week, I thought it was a fruit jam because what else could it be, right? I was wrong.

One day I decided to try what I saw so many people luxuriously biting into. So I walked into a local cafe, pointed to a piece of that bread in the case, and asked for a cortado to go with it. The man said, "Un cortado y pan con tomate?" "Sí!" Wait, isn't tomate Spanish for tomato?

Tomato bread is simply toasted bread rubbed with fresh garlic and ripe tomato, then drizzled with olive oil and a bit of salt. It can be eaten by itself but is often topped with cheese, ham or sausage. It resembles Italian bruschetta but the main difference lies right in the use of tomato in the Catalan version, which allows the bread to soften thanks to the sauce made with oil and tomato juice.

According to my local cafe owner, the original idea behind the dish was the necessity of making stale bread edible so it wouldn't have to be thrown away. It was liked so much that it became a staple in Spanish cuisine!

MIGAS

½ pound cornbread

2 pounds black-eyed peas – cooked or canned

2 ½ pounds cabbage – shredded

1 garlic clove – minced

½ teaspoon salt

2 tablespoons olive oil

1. Pull apart the cornbread into small pieces.

2. In a flat frying pan on medium heat, add the olive oil and garlic and sauté for a minute until fragrant.

3. Add the cornbread and stir the bread until toasted.

4. Add the cabbage and black-eyed peas, mix well in the pan and let the cabbage cook slightly.

5. Remove from heat, plate and serve!

Portuguese Migas is a traditional dish usually made with left-over bread of sorts and typically with the addition of kale.
This recipe was given to me by Chef Joaquim Saragga Leal, head chef and owner of Taberna Sal Grosso in Lisbon, Portugal. It's a simple yet satisfying rustic dish that can be the start or accompaniment to your meal. I've made this on several occasions with different types of bread and have also added chopped sausage. It's a great base to modify to your liking!

"Broa" or Portuguese cornbread

Zucchini Feta Fritters

2 cups zucchini – grated and squeezed

½ cup of feta – crumbled

2 garlic cloves – finely minced

2 green onions – sliced

¼ cup mint – chopped

¼ cup dill – chopped

½ cup parsley – chopped

1 egg – lightly beaten

½ cup flour

½ cup breadcrumbs

Salt and pepper to taste

Oil, for frying

Zucchini Feta Fritters with fava bean dip

1. In a large bowl, mix the zucchini, feta, garlic, green onions, herbs, and egg and season with salt and pepper.

2. Mix in enough flour and breadcrumbs that you can work with the mixture to form balls.

3. Form the mixture into balls and dust in flour.

4. In a deep frying pan on high heat, add the oil and allow the oil to warm until a dusting of flour starts sizzling when added – the oil is then ready.

5. Fry the balls in oil until golden brown and set aside to cool.

Called Kolokithokeftedes in Greece, these are the most delicious pub grub that I've ever had! The perfect snack, appetizer, or even a full meal – you can have these at any time of day.

The blue streets of Chefchaouen, Morocco

MOROCCAN GOAT CHEESE BRIWAT

1 pound goat cheese

1 egg yolk

1 garlic clove

1 tablespoon
parsley – chopped

1 egg – beaten

1 tablespoon butter – melted

Warka sheets, phyllo dough
or spring roll wrappers*

1 tablespoon flour

Black pepper to taste

Red chili pepper to
taste (optional)

Salt to taste

*Warka sheets are also called pastilla
pastry traditionally found in Middle
Eastern stores.

Locals in Morocco enjoy Briwat in both a
cigar and triangular shape as shown here

1. Make the filling by mixing all of the ingredients except for the
   wrappers and flour. Mash together the mixture until smooth and
   all of the ingredients are evenly incorporated.

2. Sprinkle the flour over the area where you will work with the
   dough.

3. Cut the dough sheets into 2x2-inch squares and lay them on your
   work surface. The dough should be thin sheets.

4. Place a tablespoon of the cheese mixture into the pastry and roll
   into a closed cigar shape.

5. Heat oil in a deep fryer and deep fry the briwats.

6. Remove and serve with your desired condiments.

   Moroccan Briwats are very similar to an Asian spring roll, however the stuffing and texture of the shell are slightly different. While
visiting Morocco, a lunch of briwats and soup was a perfect change
after days and days of heavy, cooked tajine meals. Briwats carry
Moroccan flavors well with their various fillings and accompanying
condiments while also giving the familiarity of a crunchy baked nosh.
The subtle kiss of Moroccan culture was a welcoming blend of new
and familiar flavors. I love eating these with a mixture of honey and
harissa to give both sweet and heat!

CHICKPEA STEW BUNNY CHOW

For the chickpea stew

2 (15-ounce) cans chickpeas – washed and drained

1 teaspoon ginger – finely minced

1 teaspoon garlic – finely minced

1 teaspoon green chilis – finely minced

1 tablespoon whole cumin seeds

1 tablespoon ground coriander seeds

¼ teaspoon cinnamon powder

¼ teaspoon ground cloves

¼ teaspoon black pepper

¼ teaspoon cardamom – crushed

½ teaspoon turmeric

¼ teaspoon red chili powder

¼ teaspoon dried pomegranate seeds (optional)*

1 tablespoon baking soda

2 Roma tomatoes – cut into small pieces, or 1 (8-ounce) can tomato sauce

1 ½ tablespoons olive oil

Salt to taste

To assemble the bunny chow

2 unsliced loaves of bread

1 cup yogurt – mixed until thin

½ cup onions – chopped

½ cup cucumber – chopped

¼ cup cilantro – chopped

1 teaspoon roasted cumin powder

1 lemon – cut into wedges

1 tablespoon store-bought sweet tamarind sauce (optional)

¼ cup pomegranate seeds (optional)

1 tablespoon olive oil

All of the ingredients, including the dried pomegranate seeds, can be found at your local South Asian grocery store.

1. To make the chickpea stew, in a large frying pan on medium heat, add olive oil, ginger, garlic, and chilis. Stir for 2-3 minutes.

2. Add in the chickpeas, baking soda, turmeric and 1 cup of water. Stir well, cover, and allow to cook for 15 minutes. This will soften the chickpeas.

3. Remove the cover, add in all of the remaining ingredients and stir well. Cover and cook for another 10-15 minutes, until the tomatoes are softened and crushed.

4. Cut the loaves of bread into 4-5 inch loaves, hollow out the centers of the loaves and reserve the bread for dipping. Brush the bread all over with a little olive oil.

5. Preheat oven to 350 degrees and place the bread, along with the scooped out pieces, on a foil-lined baking pan. Place in the oven to toast.

6. When the bread turns golden brown, remove from the oven and place on individual serving dishes.

7. Scoop in the chickpea stew (called chole in Hindi) and drizzle with yogurt. Sprinkle with roasted cumin powder, onions, cucumber, cilantro, tamarind sauce, and pomegranate seeds.

8. Garnish with lemon wedges and serve immediately with the scooped out bread pieces.

Migrant workers from India were brought to South Africa to work on sugarcane plantations in the present day Durban area. The Indians brought over their daily ritual of eating curry and roti, a wheat-based flatbread. Being required to bring lunch to work inspired the Indian immigrants to create Bunny Chow. This meal made it easier for the slave community to carry a curry to work without it leaking into a mess, supported within a half, quarter or full loaf of bread.

Whatever story variations exist about its origins, the part that remains consistent is that Bunny Chow turned curry into a hand-held meal. I tried Bunny Chow while in South Africa and this version immediately came to my mind–filling the hollowed-out bread with a chickpea stew!

CIG KOFTE

2 cups fine bulgur

1 cup walnuts

1 ½ cups onions – chopped

5 garlic cloves – peeled

½ cup pomegranate molasses (or reduced concentrate)

4 tablespoons Turkish Urfa Biber (isot) or ancho chili powder

5 cups diced tomatoes – fresh or canned

2 slices stale bread

1 tablespoon tomato paste

1 tablespoon red pepper paste (optional)

1 tablespoon cumin

1 teaspoon salt

½ cup olive oil

Garnishes

Parsley – finely chopped

Green onion – finely chopped

1. Place the tomatoes in a food processor and puree them or finely grate them using a hand grater.

2. Rinse the bulgur under cold water in a wire strainer for a few minutes. Drain it and put it in a large mixing bowl along with the tomato puree. Mix together well, cover the bowl, and set it aside for about 1 hour until the bulgur is softened.

3. Put the onions, garlic, stale bread, and walnuts in the food processor. Grind the mixture until a powdery mixture forms.

4. Add this mixture to the tomato and bulgur along with the rest of the ingredients. Wearing rubber gloves, knead the mixture until all the ingredients are well combined.

5. Divide the mixture into portions small enough to fit inside the food processor. Process each portion until smooth and remove to a large bowl.

6. Combine all of the processed portions together in a large bowl and continue to knead until it all has a smooth consistency.

7. Cover the bowl with an airtight seal and set aside for at least 5 hours or overnight until ready to eat.

This is a vegetarian take on the classic Turkish steak tartare. The vegetarian version has become more popular throughout Turkey due to a broader awareness of food-related health issues. If this version is kneaded for a longer period of time, the texture is so similar to the meat version that you won't even miss the steak!

Traditionally, these are rolled into fingerprint shapes and wrapped in lettuce. I like to roll them into discs and have them on crackers, maybe with a bit of a spicy sauce and fresh lemon. You won't even miss the meat from the original dish!

A Turkish lamp shop in Istanbul, Turkey

Tian de Courgettes Au Riz

2 ½ pounds zucchini

½ cup plain rice

1 cup onions – minced

3 garlic cloves – minced

2 tablespoons flour

About ½ cup milk (you may need more)

1 cup grated Parmesan

1 cup freshly crumbled bacon (optional)

1 tablespoon butter (to grease the baking dish)

2 tablespoons olive oil

Salt and pepper to taste

1. Cut off the stems of the zucchini and grate using a grater. Place the grated zucchini in a colander over a bowl to collect the juices from the zucchini.

2. Add 2 teaspoons of salt and mix. Let the zucchini sit in the colander for at least 10 minutes.

3. Squeeze the zucchini using your hands and let the juices collect in the bowl. Set aside the zucchini juice for later use.

4. Lay the zucchini on a paper towel as you go so all of the moisture is caught.

5. While the zucchini is drying, boil the rice in water with salt for about 5 minutes, drain and set aside.

6. Preheat oven to 425 degrees.

7. In a large frying pan, add 1 tablespoon of oil and sauté the onions in the oil until slightly browned.

8. Stir in the dried zucchini and garlic and stir until the zucchini is slightly tender, about 5 minutes.

9. Add the flour and stir. Remove from heat.

10. Add enough milk to the zucchini juice to yield 2 ½ cups of liquid.

11. Gradually add the zucchini and milk mixture to the pan and stir.

12. Return to the heat again and bring to a simmer while stirring. Once a simmer is reached, remove from the heat again.

13. Stir in the blanched rice and about 3 tablespoons of cheese, and a pinch of black pepper. Taste for seasoning and add more salt or pepper as desired. Keep in mind that there will be more Parmesan cheese added later which is quite salty.

14. Empty the mixture into a heavily buttered baking dish or cast iron skillet, sprinkle the remaining cheese, crumbled bacon (optional), and 1 tablespoon of oil on top.

15. Set the tian in the oven and bake until the top is golden brown and bubbling.

16. Remove, let cool, and serve!

This Provençal dish, with a wonderfully creamy texture of finely chopped vegetables and rice, is a perfect side for a steak or any meaty meal. Some even eat this tian along with a salad, or ratatouille for a Provençal mini-feast!

Stairway leading to the water of an old village in Provence, France

Amritsari Kulcha

3 cups white flour

3 tablespoons yogurt

⅓ teaspoon baking soda

½ teaspoon baking powder

1 teaspoon sugar

1 teaspoon carom seeds
(or cumin seeds)

¾ teaspoon salt,
adjust to taste

1 tablespoon vegetable oil

Warm water as needed

For the filling

4 boiled potatoes

½ teaspoon salt or
according to the taste

1-2 green chilis – chopped

1 (1-inch) knob of
ginger – grated

½ teaspoon Amchoor
(mango) powder

1 teaspoon coriander
powder

1-2 pinches red chili powder

¼ teaspoon garam masala

1 tablespoon coriander
leaves – chopped

1. To make the dough, mix the flour with yogurt, baking soda, baking powder, salt, and sugar. Mix the ingredients well with your hands.

2. Knead the flour with enough warm water to make a smooth dough.

3. Apply oil to the dough and set aside in a deep pan.

4. Cover the bowl with a clean towel and keep it in a warm place. Within 3-4 hours the dough will rise. Loosely knead the dough once again, cover, and keep aside.

5. While the dough is rising, prepare the filling. In a medium-sized mixing bowl, peel and mash the boiled potatoes.

6. Add salt, green chili, ginger, coriander powder, amchoor powder, red chili powder, garam masala, and coriander leaves. Mix all of the spices well with the mashed potatoes. Keep aside.

7. To make the kulcha, make 8-10 round balls of the dough. Make an equal amount of small balls of the potato mixture as well.

8. On a floured surface, roll one ball of the dough into a flat disc 3 inches in diameter.

9. Put the potato mixture ball on the dough disc and press it with hands so the potato flattens onto the dough.

10. Fold and close the disc from all the sides to make a closed pouch.

11. Dust the pouch with flour and flip the pouch over so the seam side is down.

12. Press it lightly with your fingers to bring the pouch back to about 3 inches in diameter.

13. Using a rolling pin, roll the kulcha into a flat disc of 6-7 inches.

14. Add some carom seeds or cumin seeds over the top of the kulcha.

15. The kulcha can either be baked or pan fried.

16. To make the kulcha in a pan, put it in a greased flat frying pan and cook it until it turns brown on the bottom side.

17. Pour some oil or ghee on the top side once the bottom turns brown and flip over.

18. Cook it until both sides turn dark golden brown.

19. Repeat until all kulchas are prepared.

Serve the potato-stuffed kulchas with yogurt, sliced onions, and a dipping sauce of your choice!

Growing up in New Jersey and living in New York since college graduation, Indian food from all different states of India has been very accessible to me. When going to Indian restaurants with family, I learned all about traditional foods and their origins through discussions with my relatives. I remember hearing from them that the kulchas from Punjab were the best. A kulcha is similar to naan except it is made with baking soda and baking powder whereas naan is made with yeast, which means the dough does not rise. Kulchas are typically made on a stove vs. the typical tandoor preparation of naan. My family always spoke about the stuffed kulchas stuffed with paneer (cheese) or aloo (potato).

Located in northwestern Punjab, India, a city called Amritsar is known as the food capital, major cultural, commercial and transportation center, and the home of the Golden Temple. Before visiting, I had heard of it as this amazing haven of Punjabi foods with flavors that can only be found in Amritsar.

I visited the Golden Temple with my mom and auntie. Afterwards we traveled to the popular border of India and Pakistan where there is a daily ceremony, parade, and party in the afternoon. Along the way, we tried some of the local food–fried sugar-laden desserts, paneer, dal makhani and local beer.

Since I was in the food capital of Punjab, I had to try a local and authentic kulcha. My mom has a niece in Amritsar so she asked her where we could get the best kulchas. Of course she said, "Oh we'll take you to eat the best kulchas, don't worry." We thought they'd take us to a *dhaba*, a local roadside diner, where we'd probably not be so happy with the ambience but the food would be spot on.

They insisted on picking us up from our hotel so we dragged ourselves out of bed from napping, threw back a drink, and were on our way to get some authentic kulchas. We pulled up to an alley and my relatives stepped out of the car saying they'd go check to see if the place is open. Five minutes later our door opened and a tray was slid in with two kulchas, a huge dollop of butter, and pickles. Dinner was served, in the back seat of the car–apparently this was a thing in Amritsar. We couldn't stop laughing but believe you me, this was one of those things that you eat late at night and remember as soon as you wake up the next morning.

The recipe does require some labor, but it's worth the time! Consider serving them on a tray in the back seat of your car to have an extra authentic experience.

SPICY AND SOUR SHREDDED POTATOES

2 large white potatoes

4 dried red chili peppers

1 teaspoon Sichuan peppercorns (optional)

½ tablespoon light soy sauce

2 garlic cloves – minced

2 teaspoons black vinegar*

1 teaspoon of salt,
or as needed

1 tablespoon vegetable
cooking oil

Spring onion, for garnish

This can be found in Asian markets or balsamic vinegar can be used instead.

1. Wash the potatoes, then cut them into similar-sized julienne sticks.

2. Fill a clean bowl with clean water, then soak the shredded potatoes in water for several minutes.

3. Drain the shredded potatoes and set aside. Heat oil in a pan, then put in red chili pepper, Sichuan pepper, and sliced garlic to stir-fry for the aroma.

4. Add drained potato shreds and quickly stir-fry until the potato shreds become soft. Add salt, soy sauce, and black vinegar. Mix evenly.

5. Transfer to a dish and garnish with scallions before serving.

The *je ne sais quoi* in this dish is the black vinegar. This lesser known Chinese condiment is a wonderful, wonderful thing and can be used to make noodles, salad dressings, dumpling sauce, or any dish that needs a sour flavor. Some compare it to Italy's balsamic vinegar, but black vinegar is less sweet, less acidic, and has a strong fragrant flavor that is warm in nature.

I serve these potatoes with lamb chops or sunny side up eggs, but these potatoes can be served with just about anything!

SPAGHETTI SQUASH UPMA

For the upma mix

7-8 curry leaves

1 teaspoon mustard seeds

1 onion – chopped

2 green chilis – chopped

1 cup mixed vegetables including: carrots, green beans, peas, etc. – diced

¼ cup grated coconut, to garnish

¼ cilantro, to garnish

2 tablespoons vegetable oil

Cashews (your desired amount)

Juice of one lemon

Salt to taste

For the spaghetti squash

2 spaghetti squash

1 tablespoon olive oil

1 teaspoon black pepper

1. Cut the spaghetti squash in half lengthwise, remove seeds, sprinkle olive oil and black pepper on the flesh side, and bake in a preheated oven on 400 degrees for 45 minutes.

2. Add oil to a non-stick pan over medium heat.

3. Add mustard seeds. When they start to pop, add onions, curry leaves, and green chilis and stir for about 5 minutes on low heat until the onions are translucent.

4. Turn heat to medium and add mixed vegetables; stir for 5-10 minutes.

5. Add cashews and stir until they start to have a brownish char on a few of them. Remove the upma mixture from heat.

6. When the spaghetti squash is done cooking, remove from the oven. Use a fork to remove spaghetti squash "noodles" from the skin.

7. Add squash noodles to the upma mixture, stir and add lemon juice. Add salt to taste.

8. Transfer to a serving dish and garnish with cilantro and coconut.

I typically like to have a simple breakfast on weekdays – smoothies, cut up fruit, or quick scrambled eggs. On weekends though, breakfast is my favorite and biggest meal of the day. Upma is a South Indian breakfast (specifically from the state of Tamil) and is traditionally made with semolina, vegetables, spices, herbs, nuts, and grated coconut. I usually make a huge batch of this and eat the rest as a weekday lunch or another breakfast (if I have the time).

YORKSHIRE PUDDING

4 large fresh eggs – volume measured in a jug

Milk – equal volume as the eggs

All-purpose flour – equal volume as the eggs

4 tablespoons lard, beef drippings or vegetable oil

Pinch of salt

1. Heat the oven to the highest temperature possible, however do not exceed 450 degrees or the fat may burn.

2. Pour the eggs and milk into a large mixing bowl and add the pinch of salt. Whisk thoroughly with an electric hand mixer or hand whisk. Leave to stand for 10 minutes.

3. Gradually sieve the same volume of flour as the eggs into the milk/egg mixture, again using an electric hand mixer or hand whisk to create a lump-free batter resembling thick cream. If there are any lumps, pass the batter through a fine sieve.

4. Leave the batter to rest in the kitchen for a minimum of 30 minutes, longer if possible, and up to several hours.

5. Place a pea-sized piece of lard, drippings or 1 teaspoon vegetable oil into each of the muffin cups in a 12-cup muffin pan. Heat in the oven until the fat is smoking and then remove.

6. Add 2 tablespoons of cold water to the batter, whisk, and fill a third of each section of the pan with batter. Then quickly return the pan to the oven.

7. Bake until golden brown, about 20 minutes. Repeat the last step again until all the batter is used up.

These are meant to be eaten right away while they are warm and crispy. In the UK, Yorkshire pudding is usually served with meat and gravy and is traditionally part of a Sunday roast. It's one of the easiest and most delicious traditional British dishes to make!

THREE CHEESE SWISS RÖSTI

3 pounds Red Bliss potatoes

2 tablespoons butter

1 tablespoon fresh thyme

1 tablespoon garlic powder

1 cup cream cheese

1 cup shredded mozzarella cheese

½ cup shredded Swiss cheese

6 tablespoons olive oil

Salt and pepper to taste

1. The day before finishing the recipe, cook the potatoes with skin on in a pot of generously salted boiling water for 10 minutes or until tender.

2. Drain and let the potatoes cool, then chill them overnight.

3. The next day, peel and coarsely grate the potatoes. Season with salt, pepper, garlic powder, and the fresh thyme.

4. In a different bowl, combine all 3 cheeses and stir well. Reserve.

5. Heat 1 tablespoon of butter and 2 tablespoons of olive oil in a medium-sized sauté pan over medium heat.

6. Add half of the grated potatoes, spreading them out evenly to cover the bottom of the pan.

7. Allow to cook for about 4 minutes, or until the sides start to turn golden, while shaping it into a flat cake by pressing down lightly.

8. Pour all of the cheese filling onto the potato pancake, leaving a small edge all around.

9. Then spread out the remaining potato on top of the cheese, pressing it down and around as you go, covering all of the cheese.

10. Continue to cook for 5 more minutes. When the edges of the bottom potato cake are golden, gently shake the pan to loosen the rösti. Then flip it with the aid of a plate that is larger than the sauté pan.

11. Add 1 tablespoon of butter and some olive oil and when hot, slide the rösti back into the pan, uncooked side down.

12. Let it cook for 5-7 more minutes or until the bottom is golden brown, adding more olive oil if necessary.

13. Transfer to a plate covered with paper towels to soak the excess grease.

14. Let it stand for 5 minutes before serving.

Now considered the Swiss National Dish, the rösti was traditionally eaten by farmers for breakfast to fuel them for an entire day's work. Every household has their own variation using different vegetables or bacon, but the staple ingredients are potatoes and butter. The key to a perfectly crisp rösti is drawing the moisture out of the potato, hence the importance of the salted boil and overnight rest. Sometimes I make these in mini cast iron skillets and serve with a fried egg on top!

Genovese Pesto Mac and Cheese

2 cups uncooked macaroni

2 tablespoons butter

2 tablespoons flour

2 cups whole milk

3 cups baby spinach

1 large bunch fresh
basil leaves

2 garlic cloves

¼ cup pine nuts

1 ½ cups Parmesan – finely
grated

½ teaspoon salt

Freshly cracked pepper

Olive oil to taste

1. Add basil, garlic, pine nuts, and ½ cup of Parmesan cheese to a blender and blend until the mixture reaches a smooth consistency. Scrape the sides with a spatula and then blend again until it's paste-like. Drizzle in olive oil while continuing to blend until the pesto reaches your desired consistency. Keep aside.

2. Bring a large pot of water to a boil and then add the macaroni pasta. Boil for 7-10 minutes, or until al dente. Drain the macaroni in a colander.

3. While the pasta is boiling, prepare the sauce. Add the butter and flour to a small saucepan. Heat and stir the butter and flour over medium heat until it forms a creamy paste and begins to bubble.

4. Whisk the milk into the butter and flour, then allow it to come to a simmer while whisking. When it reaches a simmer, the sauce will thicken. Remove the sauce from the heat.

5. Whisk 1 cup Parmesan and pesto into the sauce until smooth. This will further thicken the sauce. Season the sauce with salt and freshly cracked pepper. Make sure the sauce is well seasoned as the flavors will be less concentrated once the pasta and spinach are stirred in.

6. Return the drained pasta to the large pot (heat turned off) and add the spinach. Pour the sauce over top, then stir until everything is combined and coated in sauce. Serve immediately.

When I traveled to Genoa, Italy where pesto originated, I was able to watch it being made with a huge mortar and pestle. That was a significant moment in my cooking career, when I saw how using the careful technique of grinding the ingredients with an oversized mortar and pestle, versus pounding, was so critical to the flavor of pesto. In order for the basil leaves to release their full aroma, the leaves must be ground using the circular motion of the pestle rather than an up and down pounding. Due to this, the process of making the perfect pesto can take some time.

The name pesto originated from the Genoese word pestâ, which means to pound or to crush. The name itself deceives pesto-makers throughout Italy as it hints that the method of preparation is pounding when it in fact is not.

In this recipe, I've made a comforting mac and cheese with it, but I also sometimes add pesto to scrambled eggs with a side of bacon to have my version of green eggs and ham!

Parsi Brown Rice

1 cup basmati rice

1 (2-inch) cinnamon stick

3 cloves

3 green cardamom

3 whole black peppercorn

1 cup white onion – sliced

1 tablespoon sugar

2 cups water

1 tablespoon olive oil (or ghee)

Salt to taste

1. In a medium-sized cast iron saucepan, add the olive oil/ghee, cinnamon, cardamom, cloves, and black pepper. Sauté for 2 minutes until they become fragrant.

2. Add the sliced onions and stir-fry until they become translucent.

3. Add the sugar and continue to stir until the onions are caramelized. Keep stirring so the onions become evenly caramelized. Remove half of the onions for garnishing.

4. Add the rice, gently stir to mix well, then add the water and salt to taste.

5. Cover and bring the heat to a low simmer. Cook until the rice is completely cooked, adding more water if needed.

6. Place the cooked rice on a serving dish and garnish with fried onions.

An Indian caramelized white rice with Iranian-style onions – this rice tastes amazing with a spicy curry to give your palate both sweet and spicy flavors!

PINEAPPLE FRIED CAULI RICE

2 garlic cloves – minced

1 small onion – chopped

1 cup cauli-rice*

½ cup vegetable broth

4 ounces fresh
pineapples – diced

1 green or red chili – slit
in the middle

1 tablespoon fish
sauce (optional)

½ teaspoon soy sauce

¼ cup cashews

¼ cup cilantro – chopped,
for garnish

2 tablespoons olive oil

*Cauliflower shredded into rice-sized
pieces. If you would like to use any
other rice, cook per instructions and
add into this recipe.*

1. In a wok over medium-high heat, add oil, garlic, and onion.

2. Stir-fry for 1 minute, then add the pineapple and chili, and stir quickly for another minute.

3. Add the soy sauce, vegetable broth, and fish sauce, and stir for a minute.

4. Add the cauli-rice and stir until the cauliflower is slightly soft.

5. Add the cashews and stir for another minute, garnish with cilantro, then serve.

This is a typical rice served throughout Malaysia. If you reserve the pineapple shell, you can spoon the rice back into the shell and serve!

SINGAPOREAN KAYA TOAST BREAKFAST

For the kaya jam

3 large eggs

3 large egg yolks

1¾ cups sugar

1 can coconut milk

3 pandan leaves (or 2 tablespoons pandan paste), knotted*

For the toast

2 slices thick cut bread – toasted

Salted butter

Kaya

Soft-boiled eggs

Dark soy sauce and white pepper

This can be found at your local Asian grocery store, however, if it cannot be found, omit this ingredient.

1. Pour water into the bottom of a double boiler over medium heat. While the water is heating, in the double boiler's bowl, whisk together the eggs and yolks until well-combined.

2. Gradually add the sugar while whisking. When well mixed, pour in the coconut milk. Add the pandan leaves (if using) and place the bowl on the double boiler. The water should be at a gentle boil. Use a spatula to stir every 5 minutes or so.

3. After 45 minutes, remove the pandan leaves and continue to cook, stirring every so often until the kaya is thick and sticky.

4. At this point, if you coat your spatula with the kaya then run your finger through it and see a distinct clear path, the kaya is done.

5. Strain through a fine mesh strainer, cool completely and store in a dry, clean jar in the fridge.

6. Slightly toast the bread so it has some color, spread with a thick layer of salted butter, and top with a generous amount of kaya. Top with another slice of buttered toast.

7. Serve with a plate of soft-boiled egg seasoned with dark soy sauce and white pepper.

This tastes best when the toast is dipped in the seasoned egg before each bite!

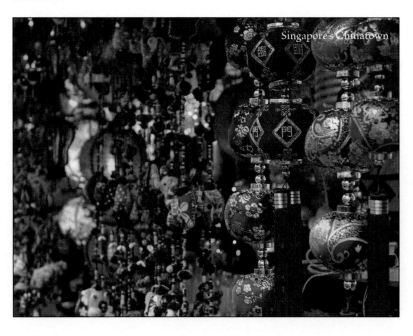
Singapore's Chinatown

When I visited Singapore in 2015, I went on a quest for a Kaya Toast Set–the rich national breakfast dish made of charcoal-toasted bread, pandan coconut jam, butter, sweetened condensed milk coffee, and soft-cooked eggs. It's a beloved breakfast within Singapore and the rest of Malaysia, bringing together familiar breakfast items of toast, coffee, and eggs with a South Asian twist.

The Kaya Toast Set story claims origins from the Hainanese Chinese. It is said they were introduced to the foods served aboard British ships when they landed in Singapore and neighboring Malaysia, and adapted the British foods into the local kopitiam culture–*kopi* is Malay for coffee, and *tiam* is Hokkien for shop, an early evolution of the coffee shop for this multicultural society.

I was on a mission to have Kaya toast as soon as I landed in Singapore because I knew I would be indulging in all sorts of exotic foods and flavors throughout the remainder of my trip. I craved familiarity early in the morning, not to mention the taxi driver who took me from the airport to my hotel highly recommended that I have it for breakfast at any kopitiam. I dropped my bags in my room and immediately went

back downstairs to ask the concierge where to find the best local Kaya toast.

It was breakfast time and morning rush hour for people going to work. I told him that I wanted to go exactly where local people go in the area to have Kaya toast before work. I was staying at the treasured Raffles Hotel because it was actually the cheapest option at the time. Right below it was an underground mall with clothing stores, a food court, and everything else that you would expect in a mall; a great place to walk around if you're trying to escape the hot and humid weather in Singapore.

Luckily the concierge recommended a quintessential Kaya spot in the underground mall where I could have an authentic experience called Toast Box.

He was right and so was my taxi driver–it was the best breakfast to have! I asked every person I met there what their recipe for Kaya toast was and all of them said the jam was a mixture of coconut, sugar, eggs, and pandan (if you have it), but what is most important in the entire breakfast is the temperature of the butter. The butter needs to be a thick and very cold slab in order that only the toasted bread and soft boiled eggs will melt it.

MASCARPONE TRUFFLE CAVATELLI

3 cups cooked cavatelli

8 ounces mascarpone cheese

2 tablespoons sage leaves

2 garlic cloves – thinly sliced

8 ounces cremini mushrooms

1 tablespoon truffle oil

2 tablespoons truffle shavings

1 tablespoon olive oil

Salt to taste

1. Cook the cavatelli in salted water until al dente and drain. Keep 1 cup of pasta water aside.

2. In a large frying pan, add 1 tablespoon of olive oil and the garlic cloves; sauté until they turn slightly brown.

3. Add the mushrooms and cook until they begin to release water.

4. Add the mascarpone cheese and stir until the mushrooms and mascarpone are well mixed.

5. Add the cavatelli and sage leaves and stir.

6. Transfer the cavatelli to a serving dish. Drizzle with truffle oil and top with shavings.

This is a rich Northern Italian dish that's easy to make, creamy, rich, and pleasing to your palate!

CHILI PEPPER BASIL BURRATA

1 cup cherry
tomatoes–halved

½ cup store-bought
pickled cherry peppers

2 teaspoons balsamic
vinegar

1 tablespoon olive oil

2 (4-ounce) pieces burrata
cheese or 1 (8-ounce) piece

Handful of basil
leaves–cut chiffonade

Loaf of Italian bread,
for serving

Salt and pepper to taste

1. In a frying pan, add the olive oil, tomatoes, and balsamic vinegar and cook for 5-10 minutes, stirring frequently.

2. Add in the cherry peppers and continue to stir for another 5 minutes.

3. Season with salt and pepper to taste and add in basil leaves.

4. Remove the mixture from the heat and allow it to cool completely.

5. Place the burrata on a serving dish, spoon the tomato mixture on top of the cheese and serve immediately with the Italian bread.

Mozzarella's rich and stylish cousin, fresh burrata, can replace it as a partner for tomatoes when you want to serve a more indulgent and less predictable insalata caprese.

When I visited Northern Italy, I met up with a local food lover who took me to some interesting spots. Our first stop was a *latteria*, which is a dairy shop that sells milk products, including all types of cheeses. The one that we went to made their own cheese on site every morning. At dawn, milk is brought to them from farms two hours outside of the city and the process of turning that milk into several different offerings begins. I watched them magically make mozzarella from scratch and tasted it straight from the cooking pot. We also tasted other varieties made on site including stracciatella which is a variety from Southern Italy. I asked about burrata, having had it multiple times and the *latteria* owners laughed stating, "It's just mozzarella with cream!"

The creaminess of the burrata cheese, tartness of the vinegar, sweetness of the tomatoes, and spiciness of the hot peppers make this simple dish an explosion of flavors!

Palate Passport

Ritual mint tea in Morocco.
Photographer: Badder Manaouch,
Asilah, Morocco

Sweets and Drinks

LEBANESE ASHTA

3 cups whole milk

3 cups half and half

½ teaspoon lemon juice

½ teaspoon rose water

½ teaspoon orange
blossom water

1. Combine the milk and half and half in a large saucepan and place on medium to high heat. Continuously stir and bring to a boil.

2. As soon as the milk has boiled for a minute, add the lemon juice; the milk will start to clot.

3. Add the rose water and orange blossom water and stir well.

4. Strain the clotted cream using a mesh strainer then let the cream cool to room temperature.

5. The Ashta can be refrigerated at this time or served immediately.

Ashta is a Lebanese cream used to top drinks or to serve with pastries. I love putting a dollop of this on a plate with a drizzle of honey on top. I serve it with toasted bread, fruit, scones, crepes, or biscuits.

Ashta is typically served during tea time alongside pastries and the Middle Eastern prized possession, dates.

Avocado Shake

1 avocado – pitted and chopped

1 cup milk (your preference of milk)

2 tablespoons honey

2 tablespoons slivered almonds

1 tablespoon Ashta (optional) – see recipe on page 232

Boats carrying spices from Iran arrive on the docks in Dubai just footsteps away from the Spice Souk.

1. In a blender combine the avocado, milk, and 1 tablespoon of honey.
2. Pour a little avocado shake into a glass, filling about ¼ of the glass.
3. Then add ½ tablespoon of honey and 1 tablespoon of almonds.
4. Repeat until layers are formed in the glass.
5. Top with more honey, almonds, and Ashta if using.

I had this shake in Dubai at a popular Lebanese restaurant called "Al Mallah". Although known for their shawarma, hummus, fattoush salad, and kebabs, I ordered this avocado shake to have something refreshing on a hot evening. The ingredients of this shake aren't particularly Lebanese on their own aside from the Ashta topping (p. 232), but the method of layering the creamy shake along with honey and almonds is certainly traditional.

SOUTH JERSEY'S BLUEBERRY PIE

6 cups fresh blueberries

1 teaspoon salt

1 ½ cups sugar

½ cup water

6 tablespoons cornstarch

2 tablespoons butter

3 tablespoons lemon juice

Pre-made or store-bought graham cracker crust

1. Put 3 cups of the blueberries, sugar, salt, and cornstarch in a saucepan on medium heat.

2. Pour in the water, mix together, and cook until the mixture comes to a boil.

3. Boil for 5 minutes and then remove the mixture from the heat.

4. Add in the butter and lemon juice, mix well, and allow the blueberry mixture to cool down.

5. Add the remaining fresh berries into the cooked berry mixture and pour into the graham cracker crust. Smooth out the mixture within the crust.

6. Let the pie filling cool in the graham cracker crust for a few hours prior to serving.

7. Slice the pie and serve with whipped cream or vanilla ice cream.

I am really proud of where I grew up–Southern New Jersey. There's a lot more to South Jersey than most people think. We have Atlantic City, which doesn't compare to Las Vegas, but offers those of us on the East Coast the next best thing. It's even alluring enough that Monopoly uses property names inspired by Atlantic City.

Aside from that, New Jersey is known as the Garden State, even though New Yorkers and other neighbors disregard Jersey as a huge incinerator, nicknaming it *Dirty Joizy*... which isn't the reality.

You've probably heard of Jersey tomatoes, but perhaps haven't heard of our other popular produce. There are plenty of fruits and vegetables grown in New Jersey that are exported to other states–blueberries being a major one of them.

Blueberries are a fruit native to North America that date back to the times of American Indians. Back then, these berries were used for medicinal purposes as well as for flavoring meats.

Just 20 minutes or so outside of Atlantic City is a town called Hammonton, *The Blueberry Capital of the World*. Aside from Michigan, there is no other state in the US that grows as many blueberries as New Jersey, with Hammonton, NJ being responsible for that title.

In 2012, I visited these farms and the bakeries nearby to buy pastries made from locally-sourced blueberries. I don't have a crazy sweet tooth, but even so, these pastries were addictive. I ate two in one day and normally I would just have half!

With some of the fruit I took home, I made homemade lemonade and oversized ice cubes with blueberries frozen inside. The ice cubes are cool because as they melt, the lemonade takes on the color of the blueberries, becoming more and more pinkish purple... pretty!

While all of the ways I sampled blueberries that trip were delicious, the best thing that I've ever had in South Jersey made out of blueberries is a pie so chunky and fruity that I want to make this every weekend blueberries are in season. After many attempts of recreating the pie at home, I came up with this recipe. I can't get enough of it and hope you'll feel the same way!

BRITISH STICKY TOFFEE PUDDING

For the cake

2 cups boiling water

8 ounces dates (fresh or dried) – pitted and chopped

1 teaspoon baking soda

½ cup butter – softened

2 cups caster sugar

2 eggs

3 ¼ cups all-purpose flour

1 teaspoon baking powder

For the sauce

½ cup butter

2 ¾ cups brown sugar

2 cups whipping cream

Plus whipped cream and/or vanilla ice cream

1. 30 minutes before making the cake, in a medium-sized bowl, pour the boiling water over the chopped dates and baking soda; set aside.

2. Preheat oven to 350 degrees. Grease and flour a 12x12-inch baking pan.

3. In a large mixing bowl, beat the butter and sugar until white and fluffy. Beat in eggs gradually.

4. Fold in flour and baking powder. Combine dates and all of the liquid, stirring until just combined.

5. Pour batter into greased pan. Bake for 35-40 minutes or until a toothpick comes out clean from the center.

6. About 25 minutes into the baking time, make the sauce. Whisk all ingredients together in a medium saucepan over medium heat. Bring to a boil, then remove from heat.

7. When the cake comes out of the oven, poke holes on top of the cake using a fork. Pour about ⅓ of the sauce over top. Allow it to cool off a bit.

8. While still warm, cut the cake into squares and spoon warm sauce over top. Serve with whipped cream and/or ice cream if desired. Store unused sauce in the refrigerator and heat in a saucepan to reuse.

Why is this called a pudding when it clearly does not look like a pudding? Desserts are called pudding in the United Kingdom. The combination of warm cake and cold cream, textured cake and oozing sticky toffee sauce creates many contrasts.

I have had many versions of this cake around the world. In South Africa I tried their Malva Pudding which comes very close to the Sticky Toffee Pudding, but still comes in second for me. British Sticky Toffee Pudding is one of my all-time favorite desserts – all diets go out the window when this is around!

THAI ICED COFFEE

4 cups dark roast coffee–brewed

2 cups half and half

3 tablespoons palm sugar, honey, or granulated sugar

2 cardamom pods

½ teaspoon almond extract

1. Smash the cardamom pods using a mortar and pestle.

2. In a saucepan over medium heat, bring half and half, sugar, and cardamom pods to a simmer.

3. Turn off the heat and allow the mixture to cool for 10 minutes.

4. Remove the cardamom pods, then add the almond extract.

5. Fill 4 tall glasses to the brim with ice. Divide the flavored half and half between each of the 4 glasses. Then, slowly pour the coffee into each glass.

Being a coffee lover most certainly draws me to try the different types of coffee around the world. Initially, I wasn't sure what my relationship with Thai iced coffee would be, mostly because of the added cardamom, but I enjoy this lush concoction! Especially because what makes it Thai is in fact the addition of cardamom pods and palm sugar. I ended up drinking Thai iced coffee almost every day while I was in Thailand!

Statue of Guanyin, the goddess of compassion and mercy, in Koh Samui, Thailand

HONG KONG MILK TEA

The following ingredients and method make 1 cup of tea.

⅓ cup Carnation Evaporated Milk

3 teaspoons English breakfast tea

1 eggshell (to remove bitterness in the tea)

1 cup water

Sugar to taste

1. Put about 3 teaspoons of tea, the eggshell, and water in a small pot on high heat.
2. Fill your tea cup with evaporated milk.
3. Bring the pot to a boil for about 6 minutes.
4. Take the tea off the heat and let it cool for 2 minutes.
5. Pour the tea through a strainer into the cup with evaporated milk.
6. Add sugar to taste and serve.

This can be served either warm or cold over ice. However, the warm tea is my favorite. The trick of adding an eggshell is what makes this an authentic Hong Kong milk tea! It makes the tea smooth and velvety, perhaps by allowing some nutrients from the eggshell to soak into the tea water while boiling.

Typically served during the day with lunch, this tea is usually the sweet addition to round out a meal in Hong Kong.

Buñuelos

1 cup water

¼ teaspoon salt

½ teaspoon anise seeds

3 tablespoons butter

3 ¼ cups all-purpose
flour – sifted

2 large eggs

Pinch of baking powder

Peanut oil (or vegetable
oil), to fry

Powdered sugar

Powdered cinnamon
(optional)

Buñuelos in Spain

1. In a medium-sized saucepan over medium-high heat, combine the water, salt, anise seeds, and butter; bring to a boil.

2. When the butter has melted and the liquid is boiling, remove from the heat and stir in the flour all at once.

3. Return to the heat and continue stirring for 1-2 minutes, until the mixture pulls away from the sides of the pan.

4. Remove from the heat again and add the eggs, whisking the egg after each addition. The dough should be very soft and just hold its shape.

5. At this point, mix the baking powder into the dough.

6. In a large, heavy frying pan, heat enough of the oil to deep-fry on medium to high heat.

7. Flour your hands well and break off a piece of the dough. Roll it into a ball about 1½ inches in diameter. Place the ball on your fingers and flatten to a cake about ¾-inch thick.

8. With your finger, push a large hole into the center of the dough.

9. Make 3 more buñuelos and fry them for 2-3 minutes, turning over when one side is golden.

10. Repeat until there is no more dough left. Drain on paper towels until you have finished cooking them.

11. Sprinkle with powdered sugar and cinnamon (if using) and serve.

The town of Bunyola on the island of Mallorca, Spain is known as a traditional village that has been preserved and untouched by tourism. This village has many local traditions and festivals, one of which is said to be where the Spanish dessert of fried Buñuelos (fried donuts) were invented.

In the olden days, on the night of October 20th, Mallorca celebrated the day of the Verge (Virgin). The streets were filled with young, single men and women, taking advantage of an ancient tradition of finding a match. While unmarried girls would come together to sing traditional songs in the streets, the men would serenade women by hiring groups of musicians and people to gather under the windows of the houses of girls that they intended to marry. As a thank you from the girls and their mothers, they would invite the musicians inside to eat donuts and drink sweet wine.

Today the festival has evolved into another opportunity for youth to have fun touring the streets of towns and cities on the night of October 20th.

I went on a hunt looking for traditional Buñuelos in Mallorca, but to my disappointment, I couldn't find them during that time of year. Though I did find them in Ibiza and was able to ask what ingredient makes Buñuelos special–anise.

Local shop owner frying a batch of Buñuelos for customers

LAMINGTONS

For the cake

2 eggs – lightly beaten

1 cup sugar

1 teaspoon vanilla

1 tablespoon unsalted butter

½ cup milk

1 cup cake flour

1 teaspoon baking powder

¼ teaspoon salt

For the filling and icing

5 tablespoons unsalted butter

1 cup milk

½ cup cocoa – sifted

3 cups powdered sugar – sifted

½ cup seedless raspberry jam

2 cups coconut flakes

1. Beat eggs, sugar, salt, and vanilla together until thick and sugar has dissolved.

2. Heat milk to just below boiling. Remove from heat and add the butter to melt. Cool slightly.

3. Slowly incorporate cooled milk into the egg mixture, adding just a little at a time to prevent curdling.

4. Sift together cake flour and baking powder; add to mixture.

5. Lightly grease an 8x8-inch or 9x9-inch pan. Line the pan with parchment paper, leaving the edges up to easily lift out cake.

6. Pour the batter into the pan and bake at 350 degrees for about 20 minutes, until cake is slightly brown and an inserted toothpick comes out clean.

7. Remove cake with paper intact and cool on rack.

8. When the cake is cool, slice in half and spread jam on one layer. Stack layers and cut into squares.

9. Melt butter in a medium saucepan. Whisk in milk, then add cocoa and whisk to dissolve.

10. Add powdered sugar; heat and whisk until sugar incorporates.

11. Assemble by dipping the squares in chocolate and rolling them in coconut flakes.

12. Drain on a rack, then refrigerate to set.

There are very few recipes that Australians can lay claim to, but Lamingtons are certainly one of them. While it's a dessert seen in bakery shops and paired with coffee throughout the country, the origins are debatable.

Every coffee shop owner that I asked would say, "It was created by Lord and Lady Lamington in the 19th century." Some say it was a sweet that already existed in Tahiti due to their abundance of coconuts, but others argue that perhaps the Lord and Lady introduced coconut flavor in desserts after a trip to Tahiti. In any case, these are lovely with a long black – espresso poured in a glass of hot water.

MALAYSIAN MANGO SAGO PUDDING

¼ cup sago, tapioca pearls, or short-grain rice

1 ½ cups ripe mango – chopped

2 teaspoons sugar

½ cup condensed milk

½ cup milk

1. Make the sago, tapioca pearls, or rice as directed on the package.

2. Wash the sago/tapioca/rice to remove excess starch.

3. Using a blender, blend 1 ¼ cups of the mangoes with the sugar, condensed milk, and milk.

4. In a dessert serving bowl, combine the blended mixture with the sago/tapioca/rice and refrigerate for at least 30 minutes.

5. Add remaining mangoes just before serving.

I call this a Malaysian pudding because I had this dessert in Singapore – at the airport of all places.

It was actually created by a Hong Kong native who was living in Singapore as an expat in the 1980s. The inspiration behind creating this dessert was to use local ingredients to make a dessert with a cooling effect due to the hot climate. I can attest to Singapore's smoldering heat!

Some locals use pomelos and other fruits such as bananas, but for me, having the plain mango version is the best!

JAMAICAN SWEET POTATO PUDDING

2 pounds sweet potatoes – peeled and grated

½ cup cassava, coconut, or tapioca flour

½ cup raisins (or more if desired)

¼ teaspoon baking soda

1 egg – whisked

5 cups coconut milk

2 teaspoons vanilla essence (or vanilla beans of one pod)

4 tablespoons honey

¼ teaspoon nutmeg

½ teaspoon salt

1 tablespoon butter

1. Preheat oven to 350 degrees.

2. Mix potatoes, flour, raisins, and baking soda in a large mixing bowl.

3. Whisk the egg in a small mixing bowl.

4. Combine the egg, coconut milk, honey, vanilla, nutmeg, salt, and butter in another large mixing bowl.

5. Pour the milk mixture into the potato mixture and use a whisk or an electric mixer to beat until smooth.

6. Pour into a 12x12-inch greased baking tin and let the mixture settle at room temperature for about 30 minutes.

7. Bake in the preheated oven for about 1 ½ hours, until a toothpick comes out clean if inserted.

8. Remove from oven and serve hot or enjoy cold.

O n a bright and sunny day in Jamaica, while my friends and I were relaxing on the beach, enjoying a few fruity cocktails, reading our books, and working on our tans, a woman approached us who worked at our resort–her name tag said 'Whoopie.'

We quickly learned that her personality lived up to the name! Whoopie was a DJ so we chatted about music and exchanged names of songs. After talking for a while about music and listening to a few songs, it was obvious that Whoopie wanted to hang out with us. So, I used the opportunity to ask her about local cuisine.

We talked about curry goat, stewed oxtail, jerk chicken and the infamous Scotchies Restaurant. I noticed her secretly holding on to a pouch of what appeared to be cake, but it was anything but that. Whoopie graciously shared pieces of her stash and we fell in love with it! It was sweet potato pudding, not to be mistaken with sweet potato pie. It is a native Jamaican snack/dessert/whatever you want it to be, typically cooked in a coal fire stove.

We wanted more, in fact we wanted to bring some back home for other people to taste, so the hunt began. We started by asking the employees of the hotel if someone could make it for us, and almost every day someone would promise to make it for a nominal

Possibly the best place to relax in the world - Jamaica

price. Yet, it never came.

One day we ventured off the resort. Just walking on the beach was quite an adventure with crabs shuffling all around our feet. We ended up at a local restaurant called Flavours and were the only non-Jamaicans there. We ordered way too much local food to try–curry goat, jerk lobster, jerk shrimp, curry shrimp, curry conch, and rice and peas.

Although stuffed, my friend spotted a group of locals with a tray of sweet potato pudding that was being cut up and passed around. He proceeded to walk up to them to aske if he could buy some. The family was just enjoying a day out and wouldn't sell it, but were generous enough to share a piece!

While we were checking out of our hotel on the last day of our trip, a really nice lady who had heard we were hunting this stuff down, had made me half a tray of the sweet potato pudding to take home with me. Not only that, she also gave me her family recipe just in case customs wouldn't let me take it!

I've since made some tweaks to this Jamaican family recipe and wanted to share with you this healthier version. I enjoy this treat with a cup of coffee, particularly in the morning whenever I make it.

This recipe is dedicated to Whoopie for introducing the pudding to us and Randy for making some for me to take home!

Turkish Delight, a chewy and nutty confection that is commonly eaten across the nation

Turkish Kahve or Coffee is a unique method of preparing strong unfiltered coffee

PASTEL DE NATA

**1 puff pastry
sheet – defrosted**

½ cup sugar

1 cup cream

1 cup milk

6 egg yolks

2 teaspoons vanilla extract

1 teaspoon ground cinnamon

2 teaspoons confectioners' sugar

2 tablespoons flour

1 tablespoon butter

Tools

12-cup muffin pan

1. In a large mixing bowl, whisk together egg yolks, sugar, and cornflour.

2. Gradually whisk in the milk and cream until smooth.

3. Pour mixture into a pan over medium heat and stir slowly until the mixture comes to a boil. Remove from the heat and add in vanilla extract.

4. Transfer the custard to a bowl, cover and leave to cool.

5. Preheat oven to 475 degrees and liberally grease the muffin pan with butter.

6. Meanwhile, cut the puff pastry in half and place one layer on top of the other.

7. Roll into a log, then cut the dough into 12 discs.

8. Press the discs into the muffin tin cups to form the shell.

9. Spoon in enough cooled custard to fill the shell and bake for 20-25 minutes, until the pastry is golden brown.

10. Remove from the oven and allow the pastries to cool completely before transferring to a serving dish.

11. Sprinkle confectioners' sugar and cinnamon over the tarts.

Pastel de Nata in Lisbon, Portugal

Pastel de Nata was a complete surprise to me. Until I arrived in Lisbon, I had not even heard of this dessert!

There are so many different versions of the story as to how Pastel de Nata was invented and grew in popularity. One of the most famous is the story of how old monks decided to create and sell these pastries in an effort to save Mosteiro dos Jerónimos, a 16th century monastery, from shutting down.

The pastries were loved by tourists who came to see the Torre de Belém, a popularly visited tower with a moat entrance, and soon were referred to as Pastel de Belém.

Today, the pastries are still sold in Belém. The secret recipe has been passed down from the original monks of the monastery only to master confectioners who make the pastry in a secret room.

I visited the bakery in Belém and stood in line to have these coveted pastries. I certainly noticed a secret room, and also noticed how many pastries were being purchased by the crowds pouring in!

The first thing that stood out to me when I had Pastel de Nata was the crunchy and buttery shell. Immediately, I thought this could be made with puff pastry. The custard interior reminded me of a crème brûlée that I make once in awhile, and so I combined the two! I've tried this recipe with lemon as an ingredient and it just takes away from the buttery, crunchy, and creamy experience that one has while indulging in these tiny pastéis.

Made in the USA
Middletown, DE
16 March 2018